KENTUCKY MOONSHINE

Kentucky Moonshine

DAVID W. MAURER

with the assistance of Quinn Pearl

THE UNIVERSITY PRESS OF KENTUCKY

Publication of this volume was made possible in part by a grant
from the National Endowment for the Humanities.

Editorial and Sales Offices: The University Press of Kentucky
663 South Limestone Street, Lexington, Kentucky 40508–4008

03 04 05 06 07   5 4 3 2 1

Cataloging-in-Publication data available
from the Library of Congress

0-8131-9054-1 (pbk.: alk. paper)

This book is printed on acid-free recycled paper meeting
the requirements of the American National Standard
for Permanence in Paper for Printed Library Materials.

Manufactured in the United States of America.

FOR TOBY AND JAMIE

Contents

Illustrations follow page 96

Acknowledgments

SEVERAL PEOPLE have been very helpful in producing this book. First, I am heavily indebted to Mr. Quinn Pearl, now an attorney in Elizabethtown, Kentucky, a former federal agent and former state commissioner of alcoholic beverages, for allowing me to draw upon his many years of experience and to accompany him in the field. Acknowledgments are due also to the federal A.T.F. unit in Louisville for some helpful suggestions. In order to avoid confusion, it should be noted here that the name of the federal agency responsible for taxation and enforcement under the U.S. Treasury Department was called the Alcohol Tax Unit until July 1, 1951. It was then changed to Alcohol and Tobacco Tax Division (IRS). On December 19, 1969, it became the Alcohol, Tobacco and Firearms Division (IRS) and on July 1, 1972, its title changed to Bureau of Alcohol, Tobacco and Firearms, Treasury Department, now abbreviated to A.T.F. Throughout this book, unless it is necessary to make specific reference to this agency within a certain time frame, all personnel will be referred to as federal officers, federal agents, or revenue men. These terms, long established in Kentucky usage, are among the more complimentary names applied to the men who raid the stills.

Several members of my present staff have rendered valuable assistance in collecting and processing material. These include Ms. Ivol Parker, Ms. Linda Resh, Ms. Gail Ardery, Ms. Ellesa Clay High, Ms. Helen McCloy Ellison, Ms. Linc Reinhardt, and Mr. William

Riley. I gratefully acknowledge a grant from the Institutional Development and Economic Affairs Service, Inc. (IDEAS) which was instrumental in the preparation of this book.

D.W.M.

Introduction

THE MOONSHINER is the black sheep among distillers. He is probably America's oldest continuously operating professional criminal, if we except colonial smugglers and a variety of deported British lawbreakers.

In fact, moonshining was also America's first chemical industry, unless it was perhaps preceded by the manufacture of gun powder. Since rum provided a readily disposable cash commodity, the importance of moonshining in the colonial economy was tremendous. Then rye whiskey came into fashion, largely under the guidance of one George Washington, and rapidly took the place of rum. Rye prospered in Pennsylvania, corn in the river bottoms of Kentucky, and whiskey, both rye and corn, provided a solid and reliable cash product. So, as the price of molasses went up in post-Revolutionary days, whiskey inevitably became the universal strong drink of the colonies.

The smuggling, as well as the manufacture, of illicit whiskey goes far back into the colonial past. All colonies, and later most states, went through a period of turmoil trying to regulate the production and consumption of strong liquors. Various local governments have dealt with the problem in their areas with varying success, the federal government having made the most sizable legal and social mistake in the form of Prohibition.

The moonshiner as we know him was a natural outgrowth of the dynamics—or lack of dynamics—of frontier transportation. Originally he was the small farmer who grew corn but could not get it to market *as corn.* Today the moonshiner is a dual personality, with vestiges of the naive mountaineer gradually being supplanted by elements of the smart, well-organized racketeer, spawned by Prohibition, and in present days often sponsored (or opposed) by powerful political machines whose groping tentacles inevitably encircle Washington.

Anyone who makes illicit whiskey might technically be defined as a moonshiner; however, this book is concerned only with those professionals whose production goes directly into a lucrative illegal market. In some areas they are undercutting the legitimate market heavily, largely because of the high taxes on legal liquor. And they aren't losing any money, either. In the mid–1950s, a high tide period in the industry, in Bardstown, Kentucky, above-average moonshine whiskey brought $10.00 per gallon delivered; in Glasgow, Kentucky, the same quality brought $12.00 to $15.00 per gallon; along the Tennessee border, where at that time it was profitable to certain nationally-known figures to maintain "dry" territory, and big-time politics flavored everything that came through a still, the price went even higher. During those years prices for legal liquor were somewhat lower than they are today, although the tax rate was approximately the same. Today, moonshine prices fluctuate so widely and so inconsistently that it is difficult to see a pattern. Forces of local supply and demand are not stabilized.

While large-scale moonshining goes on in several areas within the United States and Canada, Kentucky looms large historically in the production of illicit whiskey in spite of the dramatic decline in production in recent times. Additional large-scale activities (also declining) flourished in the more isolated and hilly districts of Virginia, West Virginia, Ohio, Tennessee, Georgia, the Carolinas, Indiana, Arkansas, Missouri, and Texas.

Kentucky was in the past and is now central to the legitimate distilling industry in the United States; this is not accidental since the licit and illicit branches of the industry developed side by side. Neither branch of the industry has received much attention from those who have chronicled Kentucky's history, and a search through Kentucky histories reveals a paucity of reliable information about the significance of whiskey in the development of the commonwealth. This is particularly true of those histories written before 1925. Hambleton Tapp's *A Sesqui-centennial History of Kentucky* (1924) is a monumental example of the deletion and suppression of information about any kind of whiskey. Tapp gives no indication in contents or index that the distilling industry even exists. The index to the biographies in this 4-volume study does not list Elijah Craig, widely believed to be the first Kentucky distiller. If the mention of legal distilling was frowned upon by the early chroniclers as indelicate, the manufacture of moonshine whiskey was heavily taboo, with only one or two writers giving it any space whatever. And even these tend to be apologetic, predicting that with the advance of civilization, the mountaineer and his moonshine will pass away.

This attitude, for the most part, continues to the present time. Minor exceptions are books by Horace Kephart, James Watt Raines, and Harriette Arnow, all written in the twentieth century, and all of which discuss moonshining in isolated districts and on a small scale. Thomas D. Clark, *Kentucky: Land of Contrast* (N.Y.: Harper and Row, 1968), in briefly tracing the history of both the licit and the illicit branches of the liquor industry, notes the fame of Kentucky bourbon, various important distillers, Kentucky's local option laws, and the threat of law enforcement. And a history of moonshining nationwide, Jess Carr, *The Second Oldest Profession: An Informal History of Moonshining in America* (Englewood Cliffs, N.J.: Prentice-Hall, Inc., 1972), has recently appeared in which moonshining in

Kentucky receives minimal discussion. It depends heavily on statistics from the IRS to the exclusion of other more interesting aspects of the craft.

Very recently two excellent books on moonshining have appeared. The first, in 1970, *The Saga of Coe Ridge: A Study in Oral History*, by William Lynwood Montell (Knoxville: The University of Tennessee Press, 1970), gives an authentic account of the moonshine culture drawn largely from the accounts of neighboring farmers and revenue agents who have raided Coe Ridge for the past thirty years. This book has a narrow focus, however, and the moonshiners presented are atypical of Kentucky moonshiners in general. The second book, *Moonshine: Its History and Folklore*, by Esther Kellner (Indianapolis: The Bobbs-Merrill Co., 1971), is a rich collection of reminiscences, anecdotes, and folklore about moonshining and moonshiners, and much of its material is drawn from Kentucky. These two books constitute the best treatment we have of the subculture of the moonshiner.

For those readers who are interested in more graphic presentations of matters, I suggest a trip to the Old Barton Museum of Whiskey History, which can be visited on regular tours from Bardstown, Kentucky. This tour is particularly valuable to those interested in distilling equipment and especially the equipment used in older days in Kentucky.

The taboo on illicit whiskey manifests itself in various ways and extends through all levels of Kentucky society. The mere mention of moonshine whiskey in either wet or dry territory tends to draw undue attention to the speaker. People who do not drink it prefer not to appear to be familiar with it—an attitude fostered by the strong temperance movements of the late nineteenth century. In areas where moonshine is made and consumed, mention of it is avoided for reasons of self-protection, and close to the still site even children are carefully schooled not to mention anything connected with illegal distillation. Among moonshiners themselves these taboos are intensified, and other taboos even more rigorous, and perhaps very ancient, enter the picture. From prehistoric times, the processes of fermentation and distillation have been regarded as mysterious —supernatural forces being called upon to protect all phases of production, especially the still and its contents. It is not uncommon even today to find moonshine stills protected by juju charms, ranging from a dead turtle or other reptile hung at the site to carefully-fashioned mannikins such as those shown in the insert following page 98. Jujus are sometimes buried at the still site or worn on the body, too.

Thus, the illicit branch of the distilling industry is caught between strong external and internal taboos, and this may in part account for the scarcity of reliable published information about it. In fact, moonshining has developed a kind of subculture of its own, widely distributed geographically and agglutinating about certain communities and especially certain families associated with illicit distilling for many generations. Often existing side by side with the legitimate agricultural society, this subculture has developed many cultural indices that differ from those of the dominant culture in several respects, including its mores, acquaintance with technology, code of behavior, attitudes toward the law and the dominant culture, and its specialized language, some of which goes back to eighteenth-century England, Scotland, and Ireland. For example, the term *backins* or *backings* is universally used by American moonshiners without knowledge of its origin in Northumbrian and Scottish dialects, where it is derived from the flax industry. *Backle* is a type of fiber which can be reworked, and *lin* (as in modern linseed oil) relates the term to flax. The word's application to distillate that can be reworked is most appropriate. The subculture, notably, has also developed very effective methods of self-protection, ranging from clever camouflage in the woods to the very skilled use of political connections. Physical violence toward outsiders has long been the earmark of the subculture, although for various reasons today violence has tended to give way to more subtle forms of pressure.

In writing this book, I have tried to present the facts objectively and not draw moral judgments relating to law violation, but rather to treat the story of moonshining as a bonafide element in the history and culture of Kentucky.

Although my approach will inevitably divest the moonshiner of some of the glamour and romance cast about him by such novelists as John Fox, Jr., and James Lane Allen, the purpose of this book is to provide a realistic look at the modern moonshiner and to give a reliable account of the institution of moonshining in the state of Kentucky.

1

LET'S MAKE MOONSHINE

Get ye a copper kettle,
Get ye a copper coil . . .

TRADITIONAL

IT'S EASY TO make moonshine. Anyone can do it. In spite of all the secrecy which has, for thousands of years, been woven about the craft of distilling, and despite the complexity that often characterizes the modern chemical processes in progressive distilleries, the basic procedures are very simple. Not only that, but the materials are so common that they are probably right at hand in your own cupboard. And the equipment is in your own kitchen. So why not make a batch? A small batch, that is. Say a fifth or two—which is quite enough under the law to technically qualify you as a moonshiner.

Where will you make it? That is the first problem confronting every distiller, legitimate or illegitimate. Probably you'll decide on the kitchen sink, and that's a good choice, for there you have running water and a drain down which to dispose of any by-products you don't reclaim. So you can select the sink as your base of operations.

Equipment? No problem. On the stove you'll probably have a pressure cooker; a five-gallon capacity cooker of the type used in canning is preferable. This pressure cooker will become your still. In fact, it will be very close to the copper *pot still* that continues in use among

1

many of the small-time mountain moonshiners. Since the cooker is already on the stove, you have only to assemble a few household accessories to convert it into a still. We'll get those when they are needed—which will be in three or four days. You see, making whiskey on the other side of the law is a leisurely process. You can't rush nature—unless you have a lot of expensive equipment. If you're of the temperament to make moonshine, you don't value your time anyway. So, knowing that you can convert your pressure cooker into a still within a few moments later on, you bestir yourself to see what you can use for raw materials.

Of course any cereal grain will do to produce whiskey, but if you respect the traditions among moonshiners you will use corn. *Some* corn, that is. There it is in the cupboard—a five-pound bag of cornmeal, all ground and ready to use. Also, a five-pound bag of sugar. This is good, for all Kentucky moonshine today has some sugar in it; indeed, sugar has become so popular among the moonshine boys that it would be more accurate—though perhaps confusing—to say that all good *sugar liquor* has some corn in it. So strong is the competition in the industry, and so unscrupulous are some manufacturers, that the age-old standards of quality are violated right and left. Thus most of the "pure corn" or "straight corn" sold by bootleggers today has very little corn in it at all. In fact, it has just enough corn to flavor it—that is, a peck or less to the barrel of *mash*. A very few throw caution to the wind and go all out to maintain the old-time excellence. These careless fellows use half corn and half sugar. Why, with corn at $2.92 a bushel, cane sugar at $30.00 per 100 pounds, and still labor at $30.00 and up per day, this is rank inefficiency! Rapidly spiralling inflation, moreover, is changing all these prices dramatically. But since we are operating on an amateur basis anyway, and the sugar is right at hand, we'll use five pounds of meal and five pounds of sugar to make our own "straight corn" whiskey. Legally, you understand, it couldn't be called whiskey with any sugar in it at all, but since the whole experiment is illegal anyway, such quibbling is beside the point.

Now what will we put our corn and sugar in? We'll need something large since we are going to mix it with hot water. A bucket? Hardly large enough since this mixture swells incredibly when it ferments. The garbage can? Yes, if it is large enough, say twenty-gallon capacity. Of course, we must rinse it out with a little household disinfectant. Esthetically it may leave something to be desired, but at the same time it will probably be cleaner than most of the fermenters used by illicit distillers—and probably not much higher in bacterial contamination than the vats used by some legitimate operators. So let us comfort ourselves with the thought that bacteria can't live in alcohol anyway, and eventually we will have a solution containing approximately 10 percent thereof.

How much water? Oh, we will need a minimum of eight gallons and we'll put in ten for good measure, right out of the tap. If we care to, we can run hot water into the garbage can—provided the water is hot enough. If we want to be scientific, we can use a thermometer to be sure that the water is well over 100 degrees F.— 120 degrees to be exact. Next we'll *scald* the meal by stirring it into the water a little at a time, and follow it with the sugar. Then we'll set the garbage can on a very slow fire and relax.

Oh, yes, we'll get better results if we have a cake of ordinary yeast on hand and a small can of baking malt, although for centuries whiskey makers utilized the wild yeast in the air and did not know about malt. So while our mash simmers (very gently to keep scorching to a minimum) we might slip down to the corner drugstore for these items. We should also buy 10 feet of high quality plastic surgical tubing, about 1/4-inch in diameter. Of course, copper tubing would be better and safer, but it would be difficult to connect to the pressure cooker.

(Actually, plastic tubing may well make poison liquor, since the hot steam under pressure carrying esters and acids of distillation can dissolve the interior of the tubing, thus releasing chemicals inimical to the human digestive system. But then we are not going to drink the product anyway. We are only illustrating a principle.) There is still plenty of time when we return to stir in a couple of tablespoons of the malt extract to retard thickening of the slurry, which at this point is bubbling and seething like very thin mush. We'll hold the yeast for later.

Now that the mash is cooking slowly we'll lift it off the stove and set it in the sink, first covering the drain with the rubber stopper. Then we'll turn on the cold water so that it will rise about the can and gradually cool the mash. We may have to refill the sink several times before we get the mash cool enough so fermentation can begin. A moonshiner sticks his finger into the mash to find out if it has cooled sufficiently. We will use the thermometer to be more certain because the enzyme that helps change starch into sugar is killed by a temperature above 145 degrees. In fact, while cooking is a part of all legitimate distilling operations, most moonshiners omit it and simply scald the meal with boiling *slops* from the still, after which they allow an extra day for fermentation.

When the mash has cooled down, we'll stir in about a pint of the malt extract and a cake of yeast, well-crumbled and dissolved in warm water. Of course, before we do this we should be sure that conversion is well underway, if not totally accomplished. This is the change from starch to sugar, which is the first step in the production of alcohol. The more complete the change, the better our yield will be in terms of alcohol. The moonshiner determines the completeness by tasting the mash, but we can reassure ourselves by using a drop of iodine from the bottle in the bathroom. If the iodine produces a strong purple color when placed on a sample of the mash, we'll know that there are still quantities of starch not converted into sugar. In this case we will have to cook the mash for another half hour or so. But if little purple shows, we can add the malt and the yeast.

Since our mash is rather thick, we had better add a little water and stir the entire mixture well with a large cooking spoon. (A moonshiner would use a six-foot *mash-stick*, made from an ash or hickory sapling with numerous cross-pieces pierced through it to assure maximum turbulence.) We can now set the garbage can in a fairly warm place, about 65 degrees, and await the miracle of the yeast "bugs," which begin to multiply almost immediately. Within about three days they will have converted the sugar into alcohol. Some authorities say the can should be covered with a cloth, others swear that it should be open to the air at all times; in fact, some legitimate distilleries still operate on the belief that certain bacteria are "indigenous" to certain areas, and that the whiskey made in these areas is of superior quality. The more modern commercial distillers, however, use specially selected and bred yeast strains for more efficient levels of conversion. Oxygen and bacterial contamination from the air usually result in a residue of unfermented sugars and unconverted dextrins because the acid resulting from contamination interferes with the action of the converting enzyme. In other words, closed fermentation with no air present produces no acid, which is perfect. Some air will produce a little acid, but not enough to kill off the yeast plants. A sizable amount of acid, however, will retard or kill yeast growth and halt fermentation prematurely. And of course, if too much acid forms, we will get vinegar and no alcohol. So if we want to avoid a bad yield and the possibility of a ruined batch of whiskey, we will cover the garbage can in such a way as to permit the escape of carbon dioxide gas resulting from fermentation, and at the same time keeping the entrance of outside air to a minimum. This may be difficult if the lid is battered,

5

but we will try. An even more effective arrangement would be to cover the garbage can with a large turkish towel. If we want to be hopelessly scientific, we'll check the acidity of our fermenting mash occasionally with litmus paper. As long as the litmus paper remains blue or shows only a very faint tinge of pink, our mash is safe. If we do it the old-timers' way, we'll just ignore it for about three days and let nature have its way.

Meanwhile, we have returned to the pressure cooker. While fermentation takes place, we will build our still. We should remove the safety valve from the top lid of the pressure cooker and force one end of the plastic tube over the nipple which protrudes from the top of the lid. Since the inside of the cooker will be under pressure when we begin to operate the still, we should fasten the tubing to the nipple with the use of a small hose clamp or a bit of heavy wire twisted tight with pliers. If we have our pressure cooker sitting on or near the stove, we should run the plastic tubing from the top of the pressure cooker to the sink, and leave about three feet of plastic hose lying in the sink. This plastic hose will carry off the alcohol vapor from the pressure cooker once we begin to boil our mash. But how will we condense this hot vapor into whiskey? A gallon thermos jug with a faucet at the bottom is just the thing. With the pliers we remove the faucet and set the jug beneath the cold water tap. We coil the surplus tube several times within the jug and push the open end of the tube through the opening at the bottom of the jug where the faucet once was. Then we let the tap run slowly so that the thermos jug is always full of cold water. The tube should protrude several inches beyond the bottom of the thermos jug. We are not concerned if the tube does not fit tightly into the aperture where the spigot was, since some cold water must always be running out of the jug during condensation. Our still will now be ready for operation when the *still-beer* is fully fermented.

Toward the end of the third day we can see that much

of the meal has risen to the top of the liquid in the garbage can to form what the moonshiner calls a *cap;* there is a minimum of escaping gas, and fermentation is rapidly ceasing. The next day this cap will *break up* and settle to the bottom of the garbage can. The liquid in the garbage can is now an amber color and is called still-beer. It is about 10 percent alcohol; if we are scientific, we can measure the percentage fairly precisely with a small hydrometer. This is the moment we have been waiting for.

We now have the basic elements of a moonshine still: (1) the *mash tub* or *fermenter* (the garbage can full of still-beer); (2) the still itself (the pressure cooker and tubing); and (3) the *condenser* (the tubing coiled within the thermos jug, which is filled with cold water).

Now we'll fill the pressure cooker about four-fifths full of beer from the garbage can. We'll put the lid on and lock it tightly to prevent escape of steam anywhere except through the tube in the top, and put it on the stove over very low heat. As soon as this liquid boils we have a still in operation, for, since alcohol boils before water does, it rises in a vapor before much water vapor is given off. The alcohol vapor (along with some water vapor and other nonalcoholic mists) rises up into the hood of the pressure cooker, and hence along the plastic tube we have already prepared; increasing vapor pressure in our pressure-cooker-still forces a steady current of steam containing a high percentage of alcohol down the tube and into the coiled portion within the thermos jug. Now condensation takes place and little drops of liquid (like those appearing on the outside of water pipes just before a rain) gather on the inside surface of the plastic tube. When enough have collected, a little trickle appears from the end of the tube protruding from the faucet hole in the thermos jug.

At this point do not let enthusiasm overwhelm you. What comes out of the tube is not whiskey, by any legal or chemical definition. Do not sample it as a beverage,

7

for it contains fusel oil and the more volatile and vitriolic aldehydes which will sear your tongue like acid, not to mention what they will do to the rest of your digestive apparatus. So don't try to drink this first product of your still; let it go down the drain where it belongs. The moonshiner calls this initial distillate *heads* or *first shots* or *foreshots* and scrupulously refrains from tasting it—after the first time, that is—though he may redistill it with another batch. After approximately half a cup of this liquid has emerged from the tube, you can begin to collect the distillate in a pan. This first *run* is called by the legitimate distiller *low wines* and is really grain spirits of low proof. In other words, it still contains too much water. As soon as the pressure cooker boils out the alcohol, we'll replenish it from the garbage can. And so we repeat the process until we have used up all our beer. By collecting the trickle from the tube, we find that we have almost 1-1/2 to 2 gallons of low wines.

Now we must do what the moonshiner calls *doubling;* that is, we must redistill the result of our first endeavor. We do exactly what he sometimes does—we use our *beer still* for a *whiskey still*. The legitimate distiller calls this process rectification and uses a separate, smaller still for the purpose so that he does not interfere with the continuous production of low wines. But we'll wash out the pressure cooker and pour in the full complement of low wines. The fire is set very low, and we await the appearance of the trickle at the end of the tube. When it appears, we are tempted to catch it, but this is not a healthful beverage either. We let a little run down the drain and then begin collecting the slightly milky fluid that appears. This is whiskey, by all legal and chemical definitions. Theoretical whiskey, that is, for liquor made through plastic tubing can be lethal. Had we used copper, it would be as drinkable as any moonshine. We'll probably get about three quarts because our operations have not been efficient, but what

8

moonshiner's processes are? Anyway, we have made some real "corn" whiskey, which, if we had a hydrometer, would hopefully show as much as 140 degrees proof. We'll now dilute our results with enough water to bring the hydrometer reading down to a drinkable 100 proof. Our final yield will be about a gallon. This distillate, taken internally, is liquid fire. It isn't as good as liquor professional moonshiners could make, because we are amateurs. But this liquor, aged, *quick aged,* or usually not aged at all, forms the basic commodity in a gigantic illicit industry extending throughout the Appalachian Mountains from Pennsylvania through Virginia and West Virginia, southern Ohio and Kentucky to Tennessee and the Ozark Mountains across the Mississippi; it also swings south through the Carolinas and into the hill regions of Georgia, Alabama, Mississippi, and Louisiana. There is also a northern extension of moonshining into New England and upper New York State. During Prohibition days the craft spread, in a very crude form, all over the United States. After Repeal it subsided to its older habitat, the hill regions of the South and southern Middle West. Now, under the artificial stimulus of high liquor taxes and high liquor profits (not to mention the high cost of production in legitimate distilleries), this most venerable of American criminal enterprises continues to prosper. However, the volume of production has steadily declined from the all-time peak in the mid–1950s.

The moonshiner as a criminal is so old that he has become a part of American tradition. He has become respectable in a certain sense; his reputation does not suffer in his own community in proportion to the penalties imposed on him by law. He is a sort of illegal pet, carefully protected from extermination by both the law and society, but hunted with just enough diligence to make him constantly aware that he is a criminal.

And in case you don't realize it, you, too, are now a law violator because you have made a batch of moon-

9

shine. If you should decide to store it in a keg for a year and deliver a pint of it to a friend who offers you $2.00 for it, you will have broken hundreds of federal laws and regulations, not to mention many state and local ones. As a first-time offender, you would probably have your sentence probated, if so small a seizure case even came into court. Theoretically, however, you could be fined heavily and sent to prison for a short term. Your home could be raided, your pressure cooker destroyed, your garbage can punctured with an axe, and your automobile confiscated if you have transported any of the materials or the product therein. You are now a moonshiner, technically anyway.

So let's dump this stuff down the sink quickly and disassemble our distilling and fermenting equipment before some neighbor smells us out and reports our illegal activities. Now that the garbage can is rinsed out again with disinfectant, and the pressure cooker purged of any residual mash, we can return them to their innocent duties and discard the plastic tubing, for it will have been damaged by the live steam and corrosive vapors that have passed through it. At any rate, you now know you can make a batch of "corn" whiskey, even though the quality may be a little less than the best; you know how a still operates, and you are familiar with the simple and age-old processes (chemically and biologically very complex) by which the starch in grain is converted into sugar, the sugar changed into alcohol by fermentation, and the alcohol removed by means of a still.

What we have described is a simple pot still operation. We might, with a little ingenuity, have made a *steam still* instead by using a separate container in which to boil water and by transferring the live steam through another length of plastic tubing to the pressure cooker containing the still-beer. As you can readily see, this second method prevents the heat of the fire from being applied directly to the still, and provides for a much more even and controlled application of heat, since the fire under the boiler can be regulated and the flow of steam reduced or increased at will. This process has certain advantages over the pot still, since with it the moonshiner can circulate live steam through very large stills, often built of silo staves, and containing several thousand gallons of still-beer. Legitimate distillers use both methods. The smaller distillers are more likely to use the pot still, producing what is called fire-brewed whiskey; the larger distillers tend to use gigantic steam stills which enable them to produce in very large quantities.

And now that you know how it is done, let's be content with theory and leave actual production to the men who make it a profession.

2

THE HISTORY OF MOONSHINING

Potations pottle-deep.
SHAKESPEARE, *Othello*

So USEFUL A GADGET as the still must, like the potter's wheel, go back to the very roots of human civilization. The fermentation of fruits and grains has been regarded in all cultures as the act of a bountiful god; distillation, likewise, was seen as a divine discovery by which ingenious man intensified drinks that were already delicious but lacking in alcoholic proof. For untold millennia the Mediterranean peoples made their wine; the ancient Northern Saxons and Germans fermented their mead from honey. The use of the still to concentrate the joys of drinking is so old that it is lost in history.

Some researchers, perhaps spurred on by patriotism and national pride, have reasoned that the still originated in Ireland—where it could have originated with complete propriety—because the modern word whiskey seems to be derived from the Irish Gaelic *usquebaugh*. Certainly its early popularity there (the British in 1556 imposed the death penalty on all but the Irish nobility who operated stills) strengthens this legend. Other more objective writers, however, have traced the use of the still through the Arabs to ancient Egypt, and it is possible that it goes right on back from there. Europe seems to have acquired it from the Arabs. There is also some evidence of its origin in China and India. However, there is no indication that any of these early cultures produced beverage alcohol in anything but the smallest quantity.

In any case, everyone labored under the delusion that the fruits of the field and the vine could be fermented into wine and that this wine (or beer, in the case of grain) could be distilled into brandy as part of man's right to pursue happiness when and where he found it. Until Charles II, so far as we know, no one among our English-speaking ancestors had conceived the idea that the State had anything to do with what was considered a felicitous combination of man's industry and God's bountiful agriculture. Therefore, while beer had been taxed under Anglo-Saxon law, distilled spirits were not taxed until the late seventeenth century, and then at a very low rate.

What gave the Merry Monarch Charles the idea of taxing distilled liquors we do not know; it may well have been simply his improvident way of undertaking foreign wars without adequate subsidy, or his high taste in beautiful women, each of which cost more than the British treasury could afford. More than likely it was Parliamentary pressure. At any rate, Charles came up with the first liquor tax in English history, and the concept of "moonshine" whiskey may be said to date from the 1660s when every distiller who did not pay the small tax that Charles imposed became what we would call a "moonshiner," although the word does not appear in English until more than a hundred years later.

Nothing so stimulates the enterprise of human beings as to prohibit or penalize some activity; hence, no sooner were taxes imposed than tax evasion became popular, at least among the elements of the population who commonly championed free enterprise. Collection of the liquor tax yielded so much revenue, however,

13

especially in the cities and towns readily accessible to the King's tax officers, that the natural temptation was to increase the tax; this the government eventually did (though kind-hearted Charles first lowered it from fourpence to twopence per gallon), and the increase not only augmented the revenue, but stepped up the premium on producing and selling—or consuming—illicit whiskey. It fast became obvious that it was easy to collect the tax in towns and cities, but more difficult to collect it in the rural areas—and the more rural the better, so far as the illegal distiller was concerned. Undoubtedly many of the farmers in northern and western England never did register their stills or conform to the tax laws; in Ireland it would be slander to claim that anyone willingly paid taxes on a beverage so calculated to liberate the true character of man. Scotland, too, had a long history of unregulated smuggling and distilling.

Eventually, as successive kings increased the taxes, those independent distillers who were discouraged by too close a contact with the collectors began to migrate to areas more hospitable to their ancient craft, and by the 1700s there appears to have been a considerable concentration of them in the wild country of Northumberland, Scotland, and Ireland. They were rugged Scotch-Irish farmers and craftsmen, predominantly Protestant, but with a modicum of Irish and fugitive English Catholics among them, for evasion of the law knows no religious boundaries. These sturdy citizens, hardened by a life in an inhospitable land and tempered by the rigors of Calvinism, or secretive Romanism as the case might be, gradually came to accept illicit distilling on the one hand as a regular means of increasing their meager agricultural subsistence, and on the other as a personal instrument of release from their bleak existence. Among these people the word *moonshine* applied to smuggled liquor, and the earliest version of the word in literature seems to be Sir Walter Scott's, "Yon cask holds moonlight, run when moon was none" (1809). The term is listed as smuggled liquor as early as 1785 in Grose, *The Vulgar Tongue,* and is probably much older.[1] Its application to illegally distilled liquor, and the term "moonshining" to the act of distilling, appear to be American developments. The *New York Evening Post* reported in 1877 that "Nelson County, Ky., is the home of the moonshiner, the manufacturer of illicit whiskey." [2] Printed usage, however, often lags far behind actual speech, and it is not unlikely that both meanings for both terms were in use in English much earlier.

There arose among the Scotch-Irish, then, a strong tradition of moonshining (by whatever name), a high perfection of the craft, a community of solidarity assuring protection against government interference, and a belief—still to be encountered among their descendants in America—that it is both morally and legally wrong to tax liquor production. By the same token, and perhaps because the king's officers were sufficiently aggressive to make forays into the sanctuary of the moonshiners, there developed a philosophy that any government officer collecting liquor taxes was fair game, and the war between the government and the moonshiners was on. It was a righteous war and has persisted even unto our own day with a relentless vigor on both sides.

Had the illicit distillers been restricted to their British and Irish domains, they would have become inevitable casualties to the encroachments of the power of the Crown; they would have gone the way of the highwaymen and the footpads who are now mere ghosts upon the rural countryside. They would be extinct. However, the great migrations to America between 1700 and 1800 brought thousands of families of Scotch-Irish stock into Pennsylvania and through the Shenandoah Valley into the great Southern Highlands, the Cumberlands, the Smokies, the Ozarks. These people were formidable pioneers. Toughened by centuries of difficult existence in Europe, the stock was as hardy as it is possible to

make the human species; schooled in religious noncon-
formity on the one hand, and politically prepared for independence by the constant battle with the Crown on
the other, they came into the new land prepared to take
and to defend it. Their participation in Indian warfare
further toughened them and brought out the character
which had already been formed; their names are graven
indelibly in the history of the conquest of the West.
They established themselves in a hostile land and exter-
minated their enemies; they cleared the land and established small hill farms; they husbanded livestock and
hunted game to feed their families, living in a sort of
half-hunting, half-agricultural society that still persists
today, especially in Kentucky.

With them came the art of distilling, not as yet illegal
in this bright new land. They pursued it with enthusiasm from the earliest days, first distilling rum from the
molasses of Caribbean sugar cane. Then, as the production of grain surpassed the needs for immediate human
consumption, they found that liquor was the most nego-
tiable form into which grain could be processed. It
could be consumed at home or sold abroad with equal
advantage, and its transportation by packsaddle or riverboat was relatively easy in the days when, for instance,
it cost $10.00 to send a one-dollar barrel of flour from
western Pennsylvania to Philadelphia. Whiskey, on the
other hand, at $1.00 per gallon (a net value of $50.00 per
barrel), could be sent for about the same price, with
much greater profit.

This apparent utopia for the home distiller was rudely
shattered by the Washington administration. George
himself at one time was a successful distiller, and probably introduced the manufacture of rye whiskey into
Maryland, first from his still at Mount Vernon and later
on a larger scale through the work of his former distiller,
James Anderson, imported from Scotland. But in 1791,
the Secretary of the Treasury, Alexander Hamilton, established the first American tax on distilled spirits.

From today's viewpoint, that tax seems piddling and inconsequential beside the present federal tax of $10.50 a gallon. It was based on two principles already well-established in England. First, each still was taxed annually on its production at the rate of 7¢ to 54¢ a gallon. There was also an alternate tax of 60¢ per gallon on the capacity of the still, paid once a year. However, the unpopularity of this first excise experiment was such that troops had to be called out to quell the violence brewing in the center of the rye whiskey area in Pennsylvania. General Washington himself, with Hamilton, directed the army of 15,000 men (larger than any single force he ever led against the British) that assembled at Carlisle, Pennsylvania. Hamilton proceeded across the mountains with the army, commanded by General Henry Lee of Virginia. The so-called "Whiskey Rebellion" collapsed, the prestige of the federal government was saved, and the principle of tax evasion, which has thrived lustily into the present, was tacitly established wherever whiskey was made. Although many rebel whiskey makers were arrested and transported to Philadelphia, and some condemned to death, the government, sensing the delicacy of this matter, generally commuted all sentences.

There is a tradition that a tax on distilled liquor had been introduced 150 years before in America by William Kieft, director-general of the Dutch colony of New Amsterdam, but this was an ephemeral problem, and a Dutch one at that.

All this happened in 1791–1794. Let us go back momentarily to the direct origins of the situation and examine some of the factors apart from the Whiskey Rebellion that made Kentucky the center for the distilling industry, and especially the illicit side of this industry.

First, from early settlements on down, there had been a universal failure in the effort to produce European wine grapes in the eastern United States, some of the monumental failures occurring in Kentucky in the

Loretto and Covington areas where large vineyards died out quickly as a result of the scourge of phylloxera shortly after 1800. It is perhaps significant that while Thomas Jefferson had imported Italian vineyard workers in an attempt to save his wine grapes at Monticello, George Washington at Mount Vernon had abandoned grapes and was producing a very good grade of rye whiskey. Only in California did European wine grapes flourish from 1640 to the present.

Second, the rum trade in New England declined after the American Revolution and whiskey was a natural substitute on the frontier.

Third, as farming communities were established in Pennsylvania and rye became abundant, whiskey took the place of rum, since the transportation of molasses, basic to rum production, was very expensive.

Then, about the time whiskey was being produced in quantity in Pennsylvania, the Whiskey Rebellion occurred and hundreds of Pennsylvanians migrated down the Ohio by flatboat and settled in the fertile bottomlands of Kentucky. Here they found that corn produced even better yields of whiskey than rye, that there was abundant cold limestone spring water (thought to be essential to the production of bourbon), and that easy access to the Ohio gave them a ready market downstream.

Last, just after the Revolution a steep increase of taxes in England stimulated the production of illicit whiskey there, especially in the rugged northern and western portions. It was from these areas that the massive migrations to America occurred. The northern English and Scotch-Irish, bringing with them not only their know-how but small stills as well, flooded through the Shenandoah Valley and into the Appalachian highlands. These people brought to Kentucky a high incidence of disregard for the tax laws, a good command of technology, and the nucleus of what became a self-perpetuating moonshining subculture.

Legends differ as to the place and time of the first Kentucky still, as well as to the names of those first to make available to their neighbors the drink for which Kentucky is famous. However, it is probable that the first settlers, at Harrodsburg, in 1774, eased the pain of frontier life and Indian fighting with liberal applications of corn whiskey. It must be remembered that until 1791 whiskey distilled for sale or for one's own use was perfectly legal; and the pioneer inventories of household goods transported by horseback over the mountains from Virginia frequently included the family distilling equipment.[3] Whiskey is recorded as having been made in Louisville by Evan Williams in 1783; on Cox's Creek in Nelson County by Wattie Boone (a cousin of Daniel) and his partner Stephen Ritchie in 1789; and in Georgetown by Elijah Craig, a Baptist minister, also in 1789. Numerous others are loosely connected with stilling, both by records and by legend.[4] We may safely assume that many unchronicled amateur experimenters preceded by some years those recorded industrial pioneers. Bourbon County, the fifth Kentucky county, was already blocked out when Kentucky became a state in 1792, and this large tract of frontier farming country stretching along the Ohio River for many miles (the present Bourbon County being only one in twenty or more counties subdivided from the original) was in a strategic position to make and export corn whiskey.[5] It gave its name to all Kentucky whiskeys made predominantly of corn, thereby distinguishing them from rye whiskeys made in the North and East. With the imposition of the federal excise tax in 1791 in the state of Virginia and shortly thereafter in Kentucky, recently severed from Virginia, prosecution of illegal distillers was begun. This was the start of federal liquor law enforcement in Kentucky. In the years between 1794 and 1800, there were 177 legal cases from 21 counties against the first moonshiners in Kentucky.[6] However, by 1802, Jefferson's administration had repealed the federal excise tax on spirits.

The history of moonshining from 1812 to the present is largely linked to the advantage given the illicit producer by the tax that the legitimate distiller must pay. In 1812, the tax was raised to 9¢ a gallon and the still was taxed at $2.70 per gallon of capacity. In 1814, the tax was raised to 20¢ a gallon.[7] From 1817 to 1861 the production and sale of spirits remained free of federal tax. In 1861, Congress passed a tax on production as a result of Civil War pressures. The original tax of 20¢ per gallon was raised a year later to the exorbitant rate of $1.50 per gallon; the next year it rose to $2.00 per gallon.[8] This inordinate pressure from the federal government stimulated frontier initiative as nothing had since the Molasses Act, with the result that moonshining enjoyed a heyday not to be duplicated until Prohibition times. Seeing the obvious decline in revenue, the government reduced the tax to 50¢ a gallon, but successive changes in the law always revised the tax upward until by 1918 it had reached $2.30 per gallon. As a pre-Prohibition gesture, Congress upped it to an all-time high of $6.40; then, in 1920, the Eighteenth Amendment became effective and the entire liquor business passed into the hands of gangsters for a hectic fifteen-year period.

Prohibition put a tremendous strain on the production of an industry which had hitherto been organized largely on a family basis, with limited local markets for products that were well known and vouched for by the people who made them. While moonshiners knew nothing about some of the present-day refinements in making and aging whiskey, they had a long tradition behind them and they tried to maintain it. Suddenly, they had thrust upon them the responsibility not only for maintaining their own local markets and supplying their own customers, but also for supplying the entire populace who had hitherto patronized the legal distillers. Let it be said that these small manufacturers almost immediately adopted the spirit of service which was then invading legitimate business, and rose to the occasion magnificently. Never again has so much moonshine been produced by so few, working with primitive equipment, in the face of shortages in manpower and materials that gave many legitimate industries real trouble.

Up to this time, the moonshiner had been a home-spun fellow, honest, industrious, agricultural in his interests and pursuits, and usually very well thought of in his community, except by the burgeoning Women's Christian Temperance Union. As a result of the sudden expansion forced by Prohibition, several things happened to the moonshiner and his product. First of all, the field was invaded by many greedy operators, who, without the proper know-how and with fantastically inadequate equipment, attempted to produce illicit beverage alcohol. The results of these crude attempts were often fatal, and the incidence of blindness, paralysis, jake leg, and perforation of the internal mucosa ran very high. We would like to dismiss all of these producers by simply saying that they were not moonshiners at all, but homicidal psychopaths; however, this would not be entirely true, for many of these individuals remained in the illicit or left-wing side of the industry, and are still there, albeit in reduced numbers. Some, we regret to note, later went into the legal distilling business on the strength of the bankrolls they accumulated during Prohibition. But most of the bad whiskey came from places other than Kentucky, and this enhanced the reputation of Kentucky moonshiners.

Second, the expanding market forced not only increased production, but an emphasis on division of labor as well. That is, Hoby Sutterfield did not simply *run off* a few dozen barrels of whiskey in the spring and a few more during the late fall, and dispense them by boat, packhorse, or wagon to his neighbors (keeping of course an adequate supply for his own family). Suddenly, Hoby and his boys were running the still day and night, trying to supply the demands of a very thirsty nation. As each run was jugged or barrelled, it was stored temporarily until a transporter could haul it away, usually by car or truck, to a wholesaler who bottled it and sold it immediately to the retailers or bootleggers who supplied the public. This division of labor is still used in Kentucky by the illicit traffic. An important side-effect of this specialization, of course, was that Hoby and his boys never saw their ultimate customers, the drinkers, and so lost much of the pride and skill that had characterized earlier craftsmen. It is one thing if your friends or neighbors die after drinking some of your whiskey. But if a stranger in far-off Detroit dies, who knows or cares? The rural and regional quality of moonshining was forever damaged.

Third, because people would buy anything with high proof, and because many of the customers were young enough that they had never established good standards by which to judge whiskey, the ethics of the entire industry slipped to an all-time low. Any and all kinds of materials were fermented and distilled. Faulty or worn-out equipment was overworked until it performed ineffectively or blew up. Aging, which had always been considered a prime necessity to make the whiskey palatable, was dispensed with under the pressures of a seller's market. Blending, which had long been frowned upon in this country (the excellencies of Scotch whiskies being ignored, if not unknown) now became the rule, the only requisites for the blending ingredients being that they make a batch of whiskey stretch farther, or that they obscure tastes or odors which preclude human consumption, or that they at least not cause the customer to fall dead in the speakeasy.

Artificial coloring and flavoring were universally used, provided the wholesaler was not in too much of a hurry to wait for this added touch. Production efficiencies fell to disgraceful lows, and have never recovered.

Last, and perhaps most important, were the social changes. Moonshining became organized, more often than not by gangsters who racketeered the moonshiners as well as the public. Moonshining became inextricably linked with rum-running (especially since much imported legitimate liquor was used in the concoction of drinkable blends), and the tremendous profits from the illicit traffic were used to promote political corruption on a scale never before dreamed of. The old-time federal revenue men, necessarily of high integrity and good standing throughout the moonshining areas, were replaced by a legion of less ethical "Prohibition officers," some of whom were both corrupt and ineffective. The gangsters who fought internecine wars for the control of Prohibition markets precipitated armed warfare in the streets of most cities and towns of the country. The moonshine business never recovered from this influence; gone forever is the honorable, simple, hard-working, industrious farmer who ran off whiskey in a leisurely fashion for the pleasure of himself and his friends. There came in his place a kind of mechanized yokel gangster who is a far cry from the fine old characters depicted too sympathetically in the fiction of the John Fox era.

Prohibition also did something to the customer, aside from corroding his innards and making him a willing collaborator in the violation of the law. While many oldsters either drew sparingly on their reserves of the pre-Prohibition liquors, paid the excessive price for imported European or Canadian liquors, or subsisted on homemade brew or homemade wine, the younger generation who arrived at the drinking age under Prohibition never learned how to drink or what to drink. The result was the Roaring Twenties and almost a decade of scandal, crime, and immorality. For the first time in America, women began to drink hard liquor socially, in public, and on a competitive basis with men. Those people who could afford it went abroad, where, pressed by time and anxious to drink their fill, they established an unfortunate impression of Americans as a whole. But most significant, perhaps, is the fact that Prohibition stimulated the consumption of high-proof drinks to a very high per capita level. Apparently Prohibition stepped up an already strong social compulsion for Americans to drink more than they should. Even with liquor taxed at its present all-time high level, there are enough customers to support a booming legitimate whiskey business far larger than any existing before Prohibition. At the same time, the moonshiner supplies a significant though diminishing proportion of untaxpaid liquor.

The definitions of moonshine vary—according to who makes them. The moonshiners themselves would define it simply as liquor that is not made at a legal distillery. The revenue agent would say that it is distilled spirits in a container not bearing revenue stamps attesting that all taxes have been paid. The general public entertains many romantic notions about moonshine that have little or no basis in fact; surprisingly prevalent, even in areas where moonshine is commonly made and sold, is the belief that it is purer, better, and less deleterious to health than any other form of whiskey. I have observed many persons in Kentucky and Tennessee, for example, who are quite able to purchase legal liquor but prefer moonshine as a steady diet. These persons constitute a considerable block of the customers for moonshine, and contribute heavily to the maintenance of the traffic. They often buy in quantity, and they always pay cash.

Most of this remarkable reputation that moonshine enjoys, currently eulogized in popular song and story, is a romantic hangover from the old days, when whiskey making was a skilled pursuit, and homemade corn whiskey, properly fermented, distilled, rectified, and aged, could be a potent and palatable drink.

Most of us alive today have never seen or tasted any of that whiskey. The demand for mass production during Prohibition soon exhausted the supplies of it. Although many moonshiners continued to make "pure corn whiskey" during Prohibition (they didn't know how to make anything else), and went on making it in some areas for several years after Repeal, the aging period for this whiskey was necessarily abbreviated and eventually skipped entirely. The famous "white mule" of pre-Prohibition days was available only to a limited extent during Prohibition. Properly made and aged in charred oak barrels, there is no doubt that this type of moonshine can be remarkably satisfactory as a drink. Pure corn liquor produced by moonshine methods was known as "double distilled fire copper sour mash bourbon," and a bushel of corn ground into meal and reinforced with rye, barley malt, and yeast would make from 2 to 3-1/2 gallons of whiskey of 100 proof or better.[9] Today it exists only in the memory of those who enjoyed it years ago, or, rarely, in the cellar of some isolated and noncommercial stiller who keeps it for his own private edification.

Today there simply is no pure corn whiskey made by commercial moonshiners, although no one from producer to retailer ever admits this fact. Today most moonshiners make sugar whiskey. Adding a little cornmeal to the mixture theoretically gives the whiskey a corn flavor, though it seems to me that this is largely in the mind of the drinker. When straight sugar is used with very little or no cornmeal added, the resulting whiskey is called *sugar jack*. Either type of drink is calculated "to separate the men from the boys" in a hurry. Sugar whiskey is faster, takes less know-how, is less troublesome; the sanitation problems involved are not as complex as they are with corn; and the raw materials are easy to get, easy to transport, and easy to handle. Moreover, the yield is considerably higher than the yield from corn. Aging is unknown. This liquor is *poured up* into half-gallon fruit jars, gallon jugs, or five-gallon metal cans while it is warm from the still, and moved directly into the wholesale market.

Compared to modern legal whiskeys, moonshine is a

potent, relatively unappetizing, very high-proof drink which abounds in fusel oil and several higher esters which certainly do not improve or rehabilitate the digestive tract. Even when moonshine is colored, flavored with caramel or other elements to make it more palatable, and aged in wood, some drinkers testify it strikes the stomach like a coal and produces lightning flashes in the brain. It carries a characteristic "whang" (something like being hit hard over the head with a hollow tin club) that many drinkers enjoy. Its social effects, compared to those of good legal whiskeys, are dramatic. Its influence on the human personality is immediate. There is no affability, no sense of well-being, no pleasant camaraderie. Once ingested, it releases the surface tensions rapidly, and when these are exhausted, it taps the deeper wellsprings of aggression which the drinker may be surprised at possessing, starting with the Oedipus complex and going on from there. After hours or—in some communities—days of drinking, the imbiber attains the state of more or less permanent homicidal torpor, and, even though rendered immobile and partially blind, is to be considered lethal as long as his fingers are not too stiff to release a trigger. Individuals seem to respond identically, regardless of sex, although the drink is predominantly consumed by males, for the moonshiners' women have not been liberated. In areas where both illicit and licit whiskey are available, moonshine is quaintly described as "fighting whiskey," while legal liquor is referred to as "courting whiskey." Presumably moonshine breaks down the inhibitions so fast that no one has the opportunity to take advantage of the situation, while legal whiskey, as everyone knows, works slowly enough to give an illusion of choice.

These things considered, the question constantly arises: Why, when legal whiskey is available, do people make and drink moonshine? There are several answers.

First, people drink it because it is considerably cheaper. Even retail, it sells for from $1.50 to $2.50 a pint, and ounce for ounce is without doubt a stronger stimulant and ultimately a more effective anesthetic than the much more expensive legal whiskeys. It is not unusual, for instance, for large wholesale consignments of moonshine to be delivered to estates and wealthy farms throughout the South, and the drink is becoming increasingly popular in taverns and saloons where a card game is kept going in the back room; sometimes, even in the Midwest and North, it is available on request over the bar. And for all its traumatic effects, it seems to do those who survive its initial impact little ultimate harm. There are many individuals who have consumed moonshine liberally throughout an entire lifetime without much visible impairment.

Second, people make it because of the high profit guaranteed by the present high tax on legal liquor. Moonshining is a craft that persists among low-income rural people who are uneducated and often illiterate. If they run a still only two or three times a year, they can have all the whiskey they can drink; if they run it more often, they can make quick, easy money. Any legitimate merchant, for instance, who could make a product for $2.00 a gallon and sell it for $10.00 to $15.00 a gallon, would rapidly become wealthy. In areas where there is a survival of frontier types, people who traditionally ignore the law and do not fear to take risks, people with little to lose, there are plenty of individuals who do not hesitate to engage in the moonshine traffic. Also, in many areas, a tradition of moonshining carries on despite changing times and changing customs; boys who grow up in a moonshining family or in a moonshining area copy the pattern of their elders, and this behavior pattern is reinforced by economics. The influences of Prohibition continue, both on the maker and on the consumer. There is still a demand for moonshine whiskey, and this demand is a challenge to those who have habitually made their own whiskey without benefit of license.

27

Last, moonshining has for centuries run in certain families who have made their livings—and sometimes vast fortunes as well—by running grain through a still. They are not going to quit simply because their activities are against the law. Some of these families have gone legal and founded famous licensed distilleries; others within distant branches of the same family have persisted in the ways of the moonshiner. Said a seasoned oldtime revenue officer: "Name me a famous brand of legal whiskey which carries a family name, and chances are I have caught moonshiners with the same name."

As a matter of fact, the entire distilling industry in the United States had its origin in tax evasion and the violation of liquor laws, first those of the British crown and the colonies and second, those of the new Republic. Since in years past whiskey making as a craft was handed down by families, anyone who succeeded in distilling almost by necessity came from a long line of distillers with a somewhat checkered history as far as law violation was concerned. Today, however, the modern legitimate distiller is one of the most law-abiding of all industrialists. This is true not only because the government enforces the laws controlling his industry very stringently, but also because he has learned that it is good business to work in harmony with the local and the national community. It is also true that today it is no longer necessary or even expedient for a legitimate distiller to break the law in order to make money since the law gives him a high degree of protection from illegal competition, and at the same time protects his market and his profits beyond the limits common in most other industries.

3

THE PRODUCTION OF WHISKEY

Be sure of it; give me the ocular proof.
SHAKESPEARE, *Othello*

THE END PURPOSE of the illicit still is of course to produce illicit whiskey, and there are innumerable approaches to the problem, many of them based on the results of infinite trial and error, compounded with some scientific knowledge and a considerable body of folklore and superstition. Each moonshiner has his own favorite recipe which he regards as superior, and most legitimate distilleries guard their production methods jealously in the belief that their particular way of producing whiskey is superior to that of others. Since we cannot examine all of these methods, we will concentrate on one as an illustration.

There are many combinations of equipment, some of which are incredibly complex and verge on the Rube Goldberg principle of machinery. In Kentucky the pot still and the steam still predominate, so we will watch a batch of whiskey run through each in order to convey a clear idea of production methods. For the sake of historical accuracy, this first batch will be pure corn whiskey. We will use a recipe which is a synthesis of several that are tried and true.

Since the pot still is simpler, we will start with such a hypothetical still of one hundred-gallon capacity. It will be located in the mountain area near a cold, clean, spring-fed stream, where the water flows steadily and wood is the fuel. Ash or dead chestnut is the best wood for this purpose, because either makes a hot fire and a minimum of smoke. Although little chestnut remains in the forests, ash is used in the form of long poles, eight to twelve inches in diameter and twenty to thirty feet long, trimmed of all limbs and foliage. It is burned green. These poles are cut in nearby woods, chained together with a log chain, and dragged in by a mule in harness. Normally woodcutting goes on during the entire stilling process, but in order to simplify matters, we will start with a pile of ash poles, carefully stacked beside the still in such a position that they can be rolled over in front of the still and pushed in endwise as they are needed for fuel. Two, three, or four of these are usually burned simultaneously. We can now forget about fuel and assume that it will be continuously available. At this point the professional moonshiners can take over. (See diagram of pot still, front endpaper.)

The pot still is a relatively simple device composed of three major units with some subdivisions. The first unit is the still proper. This is a more or less cylindrical container with a large drain cock at the bottom and an opening a foot or more in diameter at the top. A properly made pot still departs somewhat from the cylinder form in that it has its maximum diameter in the middle with a smaller diameter at each end. Actually, it is the union of two truncated cones; each half is built separately and the two halves are then riveted together at the center. However, some stills today are simply cylindrical containers made of sheet copper. Small moonshiners sometimes use steel drums as a base, but these are not satisfactory because whiskey produced on steel is not good.

Copper sheet, therefore, is basic to the construction of all good pot stills. In the old days, stills were made by skilled gypsy metalsmiths who traveled across Kentucky in caravans and stopped for anyone who wished copperwork done. The customers ranged from small moonshiners to small legitimate distilleries where steam stills were not used and, in fact, not yet known. Tradition holds that the gypsies camped at a given location and were surrounded by a rail fence which was guarded by a man on horseback. This was done to protect loose property in the vicinity. They worked within this enclosure until their contract was completed, at which point they were paid and released to go on to the next smithing job. One of their stills occasionally turns up in an isolated region, beautifully made and quite serviceable after several generations of use.

A primitive homemade variation of the pot still was sometimes made by sawing a barrel in two at a point where its diameter is roughly equal to the diameter of the kind of large copper kettle used in preserving fruit or for making apple butter. The still-beer was put into the copper kettle, and the wooden half-barrel, with appropriate pipe-fittings, was inverted and fitted into the kettle to constitute the remainder of the still. Sometimes the joint between the rim of the barrel and the rim of the kettle was sealed with rye paste. These crude but fairly effective devices are still occasionally encountered in isolated areas.

Moonshiners set the conventional copper still with appropriate fittings atop a piece of heavy steel boilerplate to protect it from the fire underneath. The boilerplate is supported by solid stone anchors and the entire lower half of the still is encased in a masonry cover with a large rectangular opening in the front to allow for stoking of the fire. This heavy masonry shell, made of fieldstone and mortar or clay, bulges far enough away from the lower half of the still-wall to permit heat above the boiler-plate to circulate freely around the copper still. A short masonry chimney opposite the furnace door provides draft and carries the smoke above the heads of the men who are working. The entire still is *mudded* securely into the masonry furnace to prevent loss of heat and to constitute a safe installation.

Once the still is *mudded up,* and the materials are assembled, the moonshiner will arrange twenty sixty-gallon mash barrels in tiers for the first stage of whiskey making: fermentation. Normally, barrels are of fifty-gallon capacity, but sixty-gallon containers will be used here for convenience. (Coopers, of course, make barrels with a wide range of capacity.) The moonshiners will be making one run, that is, they'll fill all the mash barrels at the same time and run off the whiskey at the end of four to five days, all at one time.

They will need approximately twenty bushels of hard white corn, ground into very fine meal, and approximately two bushels of malt, though various operators will use more or less according to their own beliefs. The malt is needed to supply enzymes which facilitate fermentation and conversion of starch to sugar and sugar to alcohol. In the summertime it is made by putting each of the two bushels of unground corn in a gunnysack in a warm place and drenching them with water. They may even be immersed totally for a short time. These bags are turned each day and sprinkled so that the grain sprouts inside the bags. It takes about five days in warm weather to produce sprouts two inches long. The malt must be prepared in advance so that it is ready when the operator wishes to start fermentation. In the wintertime, sprouting will take place inside a house or another building such as a tobacco barn where heat is available. Again the corn will be sprinkled and turned each day so that it has equal exposure to moisture and warmth. Or the sacks of corn may be buried under a manure pile, kept moist for four or five days, and induced to sprout by the heat of the manure. When the grain is sprouted, it is spread out in the sun and dried, after which it is put through an ordinary food chopper and ground to the consistency of very coarse meal. Larger operators may use a sausage grinder for producing large quantities of malt, which when properly dried can be stored for some time under refrigeration. Small operators like to make fresh malt for each batch of whiskey and often keep a food chopper at the site of the still. Formerly, all malt was made at home or at the still by the moonshiner, but today he often purchases his malt from commercial sources in five- or ten-pound bags. Legal distillers commonly use a wheat- or barley-based malt because it produces more enzymes. There are rare moonshiners who also use barley malt.

Now that the malt is prepared and the still *set up*, the moonshiners will fill the still with spring water or creek water and build a fire in the firebox. They have removed the cap and the copper arm leading from the top of the still, and are working through the round opening at the top. When the water comes to a boil, they will feed a bushel of the meal into the still and cook it for about half an hour. Meanwhile, the mash barrels have been arranged side by side in a double row near the still and near the source of water, which may be piped in through a hose to facilitate distribution. Now they open the drain cock and distribute the boiled mash evenly among the twenty barrels, adding about a peck of raw meal to each and stirring thoroughly with the mash-stick. This process is called scalding and prepares the meal for fermentation. The scalding is important since yeast cannot effectively convert the starch in corn without the formation of enzymes, which are released when the hot water brings some of the starch from the grain into solution with the malt. The moonshiners will let the barrels stand for several hours, and divide the remaining meal among them so that each receives about one bushel in all. After fermentation has started, they'll add water to fill each barrel to within a foot or less of the top. A liberal supply of the dried malt (half a peck) is then added to the slurry in each barrel and everything is stirred thoroughly with the mash-stick.

Although this mixture could very well ferment from the wild yeast cells in the air, a moonshiner adds yeast in a quantity more than sufficient to guarantee rapid fermentation, using several cakes of ordinary household yeast or a half-pound of commercial brewer's yeast. In the old days he kept a yeast culture like that used to make sourdough bread and added the water from boiled potatoes each time he poured some out of his yeast jug.

Now that the mash has been *set*, the barrels are covered with a tarpaulin or other material to maintain an even temperature and keep out livestock which might be attracted to the fermenting grain. For the next four or five days, the moonshiners have little actual work to do on this run of whiskey, though they may be very busy cleaning barrels, setting mash, and cutting wood in preparation for subsequent runs. Two or three times a day they must remove the cover and stir the mash thoroughly to expose all grain particles to the yeast plants and to break up the cap that forms each day on the surface of the mash. This is a thick, frothy accumulation of grain particles that rise to the surface as fermentation surrounds each particle with carbon dioxide gas. It is important to break up the cap and reexpose the particles of grain to the fermenting material below to complete the process of conversion. Some moonshiners put a few handfuls of unground rye into each barrel in the belief that it forms a stiffer and more durable cap, which they think is "eaten away" by the alcohol as it forms. There is some scientific justification for this since rye provides a superior growth matrix for yeast, although it contains less starch than corn. Its effect on the yield, therefore, is indirect. Others add small quantities of various substances or compounds, the nature of which is kept secret in the belief that they produce a better yield.

The relationship of the beer cap to good whiskey must remain a controversial question.

The temperature controls the speed of fermentation, which progresses more rapidly in summer than in winter. In winter, the barrels may be buried in the earth or in leaves to preserve a uniform temperature. In about five days, the cap will sink, indicating that carbon dioxide is no longer being generated to float the particles and that the alcohol content is strong enough to have killed off the yeast bugs. The barrels are now full of still-beer, which is ready to be put through the still. This should be done within the space of a day before oxygen begins to produce acetic acid in the beer.

Now that a run of beer is coming up, the moonshiners plan to arrive very early at the still, preferably around daybreak. Great caution must be exercised at this point because, should federal agents be in the vicinity, they will raid the still when it is producing whiskey to have the best case in court possible. The first step is to build a small fire in the masonry firebox under the still, gradually feeding it with larger sticks until the logs can be ignited. Meanwhile, about eighty or eighty-five gallons of still-beer must be poured by hand or pumped into the still at the top, after the drain cock at the bottom is closed. Now, one man has to reach over the top of the still, or stand on a barrel, and stir the beer steadily with a mash-stick to prevent scorching or sticking as the beer heats. When the beer boils vigorously, he will fit a large copper *cap* over the opening, and seal the joint with a stiff paste made from finely ground rye flour. This paste will harden as the heat increases to make a very effective seal which can easily be broken when the still is recharged. Sometimes the cap is strapped down with a metal band or heavy webbing strap, or weighted down with a rock hung in a wire or rope sling. However, this joint must not be so tight that it cannot blow apart if the steam pressure rises too high. It constitutes a kind of

35

crude safety valve. Several feet of copper pipe emerge from the top of the cap; this pipe should enter the top of a small barrel set on a platform high enough to keep it level with the still-cap. Someone puts a few gallons of fresh still-beer into this barrel, and the still is ready to go into action.

As the fire builds up, the beer inside the still heats and eventually boils. Hot steam, bearing more alcohol than water, moves from the still through the copper pipe into the barrel, the copper pipe reaching to a point about four inches off the barrel floor. This steam passes through the still-beer, heating it almost to the boiling point, and emerges from the top of the beer in bubbles whose characteristic sound gives the barrel its name: *thump-keg*. Some moonshiners in Kentucky operate with a dry thump-keg or one that contains only the small amount of liquid condensing from the passing vapor. Within the thump-keg the vapor is redistilled by its own heat, yielding a higher-proof distillate than could normally be obtained without its use. Another copper pipe emerges from the opposite side of the top of this barrel and carries the live steam several feet farther to the *flakestand*. The flakestand consists of a steel drum or wooden barrel with the top knocked out and a supply of cold spring water running into the top and overflowing when the barrel is full. This barrel is mounted securely on a masonry or timber foundation at about the same height as the thump-keg. Copper piping that transmits the steam from the thump-keg passes into the open top of this barrel. There the pipe becomes a coil that stands upright in the barrel, with the end of the copper tubing protruding from the lower portion of the barrel for a distance of several inches. (While this is the most common form of the coil, there are endless variations in the shape and form of the condenser.) The copper coil is usually made separately by nailing the end of a length of copper tubing to the bottom of a tree eight or ten inches in diameter. The tubing is then wrapped around the tree for eight or ten turns and cut off at the desired length. (The pipe may be first filled with sand to reduce flattening during this wrapping process.) The tree is sawed down, the bottom of the copper tubing cut loose, and the coil slipped from the tree. Fittings are then attached so that the end of the copper coil can be connected to the pipe entering the flakestand at the top, and the lower end of the coil can be supported on the bottom of the flakestand. A shutoff valve may or may not be used on the end of the copper tubing protruding from the flakestand, and the aperture through which the tube passes may be crudely sealed. As the steam bubbles to the surface of the backings in the thump-keg, passing through the copper pipe into the flakestand, its progress is slowed down by the cold flowing spring water that surrounds the pipe, and sudden condensation takes place within the coil. At this point the fire should be tended carefully so that regular, optimal heat is available. The first liquid appearing from the flakestand will be the foreshots. Largely consisting of fusel oil and very undesirable esters which are not palatable and can even be lethal, the foreshots are usually discarded, though some moonshiners pour them into the thump-keg to reclaim any alcohol they contain. The still hands will put a container called a *catch-can* under the end of the copper tubing to catch the whiskey as it emerges, and set it aside when the alcohol is exhausted from the still. At this point, they open the drain cock at the bottom and release the spent mash. Then they draw or bank the fire, remove the still-cap, close the drain cock, fill the still with fresh beer, replace the cap, seal it, increase the fire, and another cycle of *stilling* is underway.

While some moonshiners use a standard drain cock with a shut-off valve, others use a very practical device made by tying a wad of rags to the end of a green sapling about three feet long. This is put into the still from the top with the end protruding through the opening at the bottom and the wad of rags remaining in the still.

The drain cock can then rapidly and easily be closed by pulling hard on the protruding stick. And it can be opened with equal ease by driving the stick back into the still to remove the rags from the opening.

When the contents of the remaining barrels have been run through the still, the operators will collect the resulting low-proof liquor and set it aside in empty barrels for redistillation. The quantity will vary according to the efficiency of their apparatus and several other factors. Some moonshiners do not redistill the liquor when they use a thump-keg, especially if their equipment is efficient enough to produce whiskey of about 100 proof. If a moonshiner wants really high-proof whiskey he will usually redistill his distillate and cut it back afterward. There is also a wide variety of redistillation practices that cannot be treated in detail here.

They will now pull the fire from under the still, which is very hot. Once more, they open the drain cock, and allow the last run of *spent beer* or slops to run out. It may be conducted through a large fire hose or metal pipe to the edge of the creek or to a sump where it does not contaminate the work space.

If they were the kind of moonshiners who operated regularly, they would have meanwhile prepared twenty fresh barrels and saved the last slops from the run to scald the new meal that would form the base for another cycle of fermentation. While this was going on, they would scrub the first tier of barrels carefully, treat them with lime to kill contamination, and prepare them for filling later on.

About twenty-five gallons of hot slops per bushel is optimum under atmospheric pressure which is, of course, what the moonshiner is using. There are many sound scientific reasons why hot spent beer is an ideal medium in which to start a new cycle of fermentation, but the moonshiner is unaware of these. Undoubtedly, however, centuries of trial and error have established and maintained this practice because it produces good results.

Now for the distillate itself. The still is cleaned and filled with low wines. The fire is built up until the alcohol boils and the steam passes through the entire apparatus again, emerging from the flakestand as high-proof straight corn whiskey since no sugar has been added. Theoretically this could be redistilled several times to produce 180 proof alcohol or better. But of course a moonshiner's primitive equipment cannot duplicate the efficiency of the precisely-engineered still. Therefore, the operator will be fortunate to get liquor of 140 proof. As this liquid trickles from the flakestand, he catches some in a pint bottle, shakes it vigorously, and watches the *bead*, the little chain of bubbles that appears on the meniscus of the liquor where it touches the glass. (The meniscus is the level-line where the surface of the liquid meets the glass.) These beads will float high on the liquid, indicating that the liquor is well over 100 proof. Good whiskey will hold the bead where it stops on the meniscus after the stiller thumps it in the palm of his hand, and an experienced stiller can judge the proof very closely by observing the bead. Very modern moonshiners may use a hydrometer to test the proof, but old-timers prefer the *temping bottle*, in which the liquor is *temped*. When the high-proof liquor gives way to lower-proof spirits, the moonshiner knows that his backings are exhausted and that the rest of the run will be low-proof liquor produced from low wines boiling in the still. He sets aside the high-proof liquor for later mixing.

When the low wines are all exhausted and the liquor has been distilled and redistilled, he will have approximately forty to forty-five gallons of high-proof liquor, which he will then cut with the last run of *singlings* or with low wines or ordinary spring water to about 100 proof; this can be adequately estimated by an experienced moonshiner when the temping bottle holds a bead exactly half way over and half way under the meniscus. Therefore, the net yield of 100 proof whiskey from twenty bushels of corn will be approximately fifty to sixty gallons, depending on the completeness of the fermentation process, the reliability of the equipment, and the efficiency of the operator.[1] While the moonshiner's yield is small compared to that of the legitimate distiller, it is relatively good considering his methods. He has little control over the acidity of his mash and seldom, if ever, gets the benefit of what legal distillers call the secondary conversion. Some of the starch in his meal always remains unconverted and is discarded with the slops. Yet, when aged four years or more, his whiskey will be smooth, light, and delicious. Unless it is contaminated with artificial coloring, it will be clear or very slightly smoky in color and may have a very faint amber tint from the oak barrel. It is a sad thing that more of it is not made. This whiskey may be run through a container full of charcoal before it is jugged for transportation. Good moonshiners also use a felt filter, sometimes purchased commercially, though smaller operators may substitute an old felt hat.

So far we have been observing the simple prototype of the pot still. More sophisticated moonshiners may increase their efficiency by adding more than one thump-keg in a series, by installing a *puker* between the still and the first thump-keg, and by inserting a *heater-box* between the thump-keg and the flakestand. The puker is simply a small keg or tank that catches any solids which may boil out of the still and prevents them from passing through with the liquor. (In legitimate distilling, a similar but more complicated device is used, known as a dephlegmator.)

The heater-box is a metal or wooden container set at a convenient height between the thump-keg and flakestand, with the hot steam piped in from the thump-keg. Within the box, the copper pipe makes a complete circle and emerges from the opposite end to attach to the flakestand. The heater-box is filled with still-beer, and the heat from the copper tubing within prepares the beer for distillation. Where a large heater-box is used, the moonshiner may enlarge the diameter of the tubing inside the box or add three or four short auxiliary tubes, each carrying live steam so that the heat may be widely distributed. These tubes merge with the entrance and exit tube that brings the steam in and out of the box. The addition of the puker, the second thump-keg, and the heater-box improves the efficiency of the still, preserves heat, saves time, and provides a regular supply of hot, fresh still-beer. This process is sometimes facilitated by running a pipe from the heater-box back to the still with a cutoff valve in between so that the flow of beer can be regulated. For this to work, the entire assembly must be set up so that gravity carries the still-beer back from the heater-box to the still.

There are too many variations of the basic pot still arrangement to describe here in detail. However, one variation should be mentioned. Some moonshiners, especially old-timers in the back country, use only a beer still and a flakestand to produce what a legitimate distiller would call low wines. They then run the low wines through a so-called liquor or whiskey still which is very much smaller and may be run simultaneously with the larger beer still. This second distillation, technically called rectification, produces very high-proof whiskey. There are still some small legitimate distillers who use both the beer still and the whiskey still in the production of high quality bourbon whiskey.

Today, of course, moonshine whiskey is fortunate to have ten pounds of corn to the barrel of mash and some moonshine has even less. Now we will watch as a batch of modern moonshine is run through a steam still, in order to appreciate the differences between the pot still and the steam still (see back endpaper) and between pure corn and modern moonshine.

The steam still has some elements in common with

41

the pot still and, of course, the principles of distillation involved are identical. However, the steam still starts with a *boiler* that converts water to steam. This boiler is usually large, placed on a masonry foundation, equipped with boiler pipes and safety accessories, connected to a steady water supply, and fired by kerosene or gasoline under pressure. Under certain conditions wood, natural gas, bottled gas, or electricity may be used instead. A steady head of steam is produced and maintained throughout the operation. The beer still is built on a masonry foundation, and consists simply of a large closed cylinder, of copper, aluminum, or wooden silo staves, that contains a large amount of beer. The steam is piped from the boiler through the *cooker* or beer still and terminates about six inches from the bottom. A copper exit pipe leads from the upper portion of the cooker to the arrangement of one, two, or more thump-kegs described in connection with the pot still. Once the cooker is full of beer and the live steam is introduced, distillation begins as soon as the alcohol reaches its boiling point, which will vary according to the altitude, the composition of the mixture, and the nature of the equipment. However, alcohol always boils at a lower temperature than water.[2] The alcohol-laden steam passes on into and through the thump-kegs and into a flakestand similar to but often larger than that used by a pot still. Fresh, cold running water is likewise applied, and the whiskey is collected in the catch-can.

The chief difference, then, between the pot still and the steam still is that the steam still cooks the beer without putting it into direct contact with the fire. There are also minor differences. For instance, the steam circulated through the cooker of the steam still is very hot, retains its heat throughout the distillation process, and may create a problem of incomplete condensation in the flakestand. Many moonshiners use this extra heat by building some variety of heater-box as previously described. The heater-box is filled with beer which is started on its cooking and distillation process by the hot steam passing through the copper pipes inside the box. A large-diameter pipe connects the heater-box with the cooker. Cutoff valves enable the distiller to allow the beer in the heater-box to flow by when needed to replenish the still-beer in the main cooker.

The great advantage of the heater-box used with a steam still is that when the beer in the cooker is spent, the steam from the boiler can be shut off. The hot, spent beer can then be pumped out, possibly into a new tier of fermenters where scalding takes place, and almost instantly the cooker is refilled with hot beer from the heater-box. The steam is then turned on and the process continues without the delay and extra work involved in recharging a pot still. Steam stills can run almost continuously if they are managed properly, that is, as long as fermented still-beer is available to feed the heater-box and the spent beer is pumped out.

The flakestand for the steam still may be made of copper coils immersed in cold water, but often a large truck radiator, which provides increased surface exposure to the cold water, is used; in a large steam still, several truck radiators may be welded or soldered together. In recent years since the introduction of truck radiators as condensers, an alarming rate of lead poisoning has been encountered among regular drinkers, since the lead soldering inside the radiators tends to go into solution in the alcohol. Of course, these larger flakestands require a much increased flow of cold water to facilitate condensation within the radiator. Some steam distillers also insert a puker.

For simplicity's sake, our hypothetical moonshiners are using the same thump-keg and flakestand arrangement that was used to make corn whiskey. They are also using twenty barrels for fermentation. The pot still has simply been replaced with a steam still and its auxiliary boiler. It is fired with a kerosene burner attached to a long pipe, which is in turn attached to a rubber hose

43

leading to a gas-powered compressor. Once the compressor is activated, a pressure tank supplies a steady flow of vaporized kerosene under uniform pressure to the burner at the end of the long pipe. This burner may be pushed under the boiler or removed at will, and the problem of heat is solved. The moonshiners will fill the boiler with water pumped in from a stream or spring or allowed to run by gravity from a reserve tank. Thus steam will be available shortly after the burner is lit. Meanwhile, the moonshiners set their *sugar mash* in a slightly different fashion than those who use corn. The barrels are clean and dry and arranged in a double row or tier close to the still. About four bushels of malt have been prepared, dried and ground in advance, and are now ready for use. Under the protecting shed there are twenty fifty-pound bags of sugar and five bushels of finely ground corn meal. The moonshiners are now ready to set the mash.

The boiler is filled, and the burner is lit to produce steam. The still (not to be confused with the boiler) is filled with eighty gallons of water, and five bushels of corn meal is stirred in slowly from the top. The hot steam enclosed in pipes passing through the still cooks this mixture for about an hour to produce a thin slurry. At this point, the fire is turned off, the drain cock of the still is opened, and approximately five gallons of hot slurry is pumped or carried to each barrel. After this cools, ten pounds of sugar and eight pounds of malt are stirred into each barrel. Brewer's yeast may be added to assure and facilitate fermentation. Moonshiners commonly overyeast their mash, using about a half-pound cake of yeast per barrel.

Some moonshiners, especially those who have had experience making corn whiskey in the past, put a small amount of nitrate into each barrel in the form of commercial fertilizer used for tobacco or corn. This *kick* or *kicker* has a catalytic effect on the conversion process and probably gives a slightly increased yield. Interestingly enough, this addition of nitrate to the mash seems to have been discovered in older days in Europe when barnyard fowl often pecked mash from the cap and roosted tails-in over the warm barrels. It was noticed that their droppings, later known to be high in nitrate, increased the yield.

The barrels are then filled with water to within two feet of the top, and this mixture is allowed to ferment for about three days or until the yeast is growing vigorously. At this point, forty pounds of sugar is stirred into each barrel with about four pounds of malt. From two to four pounds of rye is added in order to give a firm cap. This will fill the barrels, leaving enough room at the top to allow for the froth of fermentation. The cap that forms with sugar whiskey is much thinner and lighter than the one that forms when pure corn is used. These barrels are allowed to ferment for a total of four to five days or until the process of conversion is complete. At this time, the boiler is fired once more, the still, which has been rinsed out thoroughly, is filled almost to the top with still-beer, and the distillation process continues much as it did in making corn whiskey.

Many steam stills have variations in structure that enable them to feed hot beer and backings into the still. This is accomplished by the use of a *relay keg*, a combination dry rectifying barrel and large *preheater box* which is tapped into the line between the still and the flakestand. There are many variations of this system, some of which permit practically continuous operation of the steam still until the tier of fermenters is empty. Rather than coming into direct contact with the fire, the steam still is fed by a strong head of live steam that boils the beer in it and serves in effect as a giant thump-keg to produce a continuous supply of backings, which are then redistilled to achieve maximum proof. From the ingredients listed above, experienced moonshiners should net 110 to 115 gallons of 100 proof sugar whiskey, the quality of which is a far cry from that of pure corn whiskey. But whiskey from these materials constitutes most of the bootleg liquor sold in the United States today, regardless of the type of still in which it is produced.

Steam stills are commonly used in the Nelson and Marion county area and in western Kentucky, although they may be found in any moonshine producing county. They are newer in concept and permit a more regular production of large quantities of liquor than would normally be expected from pot stills of comparable size. However, the steam still also presents logistic problems such as the regular ingress of raw materials and fuels.

Pot stills are used mainly in the eastern mountains as well as along the Tennessee border, though they also may appear side by side with steam stills. Pot stills are the older, traditional type of moonshine equipment and are often preferred by older men. It is not uncommon to encounter a skilled old-time whiskey maker who does not know how to build or operate a steam still, although of course he knows about their use.

4

THE GEOGRAPHY OF MOONSHINING

The gods sent not corn
for the rich men only.
SHAKESPEARE, *Coriolanus*

THE FACT THAT Kentucky has long been the center of
the illegal distilling business might lead some to the
conclusion that moonshining activity is limited to this
state alone. Actually, there is considerable moonshine
production in most of the fifty states. One phase of the
moonshine industry that is often and easily overlooked
is an extension into the northern states from the southeastern section of the country that encompasses Kentucky, Tennessee, the Carolinas, Alabama, Mississippi,
Georgia, Virginia, and West Virginia. Even in Oklahoma
and Texas there are scattered pockets of well-en-
trenched moonshine activity, due to the continued migration of the people of Appalachia to the Southwest.

Nonetheless, the region encompassing the southeastern states produces far more moonshine than all the
other states combined,[1] and most of the illicit operations
outside this concentration are in the neighboring communities of Southern Indiana, Ohio, Missouri, Arkansas
(in the Ozarks), Illinois, and especially the area in
southern Illinois called Egypt, at the confluence of the
Ohio and Mississippi rivers.

47

It is not difficult to explain, superficially at least, why the moonshine industry should have flourished historically in the southeastern region, bounded on the west by the Mississippi River and on the north by the Ohio. Specifically, this is the legal whiskey manufacturing area, and so both bootlegging and transporting of illicit spirits are most common here. Possibly some of this illegal activity may be explained by the traditions and proclivities of the European peoples who first settled in this area; much of it in Kentucky certainly results from the region's proximity to the area of concentration of legitimate distillers. But to isolate a single reason for the concentration of illegal distilling would be to oversimplify a problem that the Treasury Department's experts have puzzled over during the years since Repeal.

A large portion of the moonshine stills found in areas adjacent to the southeastern region are manned by, owned by, or financed by moonshiners from the southeastern states. This occurs for several reasons. Sometimes the moonshiners get "hot" in their native habitats and move to surroundings where their names, their reputations, their faces, and their habits are not so well-known to the officers. Shortly prior to this writing, for example, several large stills were seized in southern Indiana and most of those arrested were natives of central Kentucky. Also, whiskey transporters from Kentucky like to compete in the stock-car races at southern Indiana tracks where their experience in handling hot cars in difficult driving conditions gives them a distinct advantage. A fast car and the hazards of the chase are irresistible to whiskey transporters, who are universally young and very expert.

A series of car seizures for transportation of "white lightning" in Dayton, Ohio, turned up the faces of other central Kentucky moonshiners well known to the revenue men at home but unfamiliar to officers in Ohio. And there has been considerable increase in the manufacturing of illicit whiskey in Detroit, which officers there

48

attribute to the large-scale migration of workers and their families from Appalachia. When these people are laid off or lose their jobs, their immediate tendency is to revert to whatever leisure activities they might have engaged in at home. Sometimes three or four will go to the basement, which is already equipped with gas, sewage, and water facilities, and set up a small still. Occasionally, the citizens of a law-abiding residential area are shocked to find that a large still has been operating in their neighborhood for several weeks. The great bulk of illicit whiskey in the Detroit area, however, is produced by large syndicates using *alky columns* and fermenting molasses or sugar.

Wherever moonshiners go, their production is likely to follow very shortly. There seems to be an untapped market for the *splo* (cheap rotgut moonshine) in most cities; and when the visiting or fleeing moonshiner discovers the existence of the craving, his reaction is like that of the well-known old fire horse. The opportunity must not be overlooked. So, letters go back home to explain the bright prospects to friends, brothers, or uncles. Arrangements are made to satisfy the demand, and the money begins to roll in. The bulk of moonshine whiskey produced by big operators is sold outside the county where it is made and outside the state where it is produced.

Interesting examples of this geographical diffusion during Prohibition days are New Straitsville and Cleveland, Ohio, areas not previously notorious for illicit whiskey production. In New Straitsville, the moonshiners holed up in abandoned coal mines and poured forth an incredible volume of rather good moonshine whiskey. In fact, radio station WAVE in Louisville announced that May 24 this year was celebrated in New Straitsville as "Moonshine Day." In Cleveland, a family of illicit liquor manufacturers (widely known as the Corn Sugar Boys) used commercial corn sugar as the chief raw material and supplied a vast market.

49

In short, although the Ohio and Mississippi rivers bound the area of major moonshining concentration, they do not contain it. But most of the stills in these neighboring states are relatively small, and there seems to be little big-time organization among the moonshiners there.

Another peripheral area of moonshining includes parts of New York, Pennsylvania, and all of New England, even though activity there is minor by comparison to that in the Southeast. The word "minor," however, carries a different connotation when it is used to describe moonshining activity in a heavily populated area like New York. Whereas in an area like the Ozarks the violations themselves are usually minor, the moonshining activity in the New York area is "minor" in that the number of violations are few. On the other hand, when a still is seized in New York, it is often an alky column capable of enormous production overshadowing the production capacity of most Southern stills. (This helps to explain the emphasis such seizures get in the press.) Also, by reason of size and the complex nature of such urban communities, the likelihood of syndicate organization is much greater.

It is a well-known fact that federal and local judges within established moonshine areas take a much more humane view of the seriousness of liquor law violations than their counterparts in other areas, and this may account in part for the continued concentration of moonshining in one section of the country. Even when conviction rates are comparable, a larger number of probated and reduced sentences is given in the southeastern region, especially to first- and second-time offenders. In spite of their reference to the Ashland penitentiary as "The Country Club" and despite the fact that they get fat, receive excellent medical attention, new teeth, eyeglasses, and education, meet other good moonshiners, and obtain additional benefits, the moonshiners generally like life better in their native habitat.

Throughout the southeastern states, there are, of course, extremes in the incidence of liquor law violations, just as there are extremes in the violation of other laws. In some communities there are practically no liquor law violations; in other communities, there are numerous stills and bootleggers, all small; in yet others nearby, the stills are large, and traffic in illicit liquor is big business, well organized, and furnishes full-time occupation to large groups of people. But outside of the tightly organized syndicates there is relatively little big-time activity among the moonshiners.

Perhaps the reasons for the high participation in the traffic in this region may be enumerated, although it is certain that the same reasons do not apply equally to all areas and that some valid reasons will be omitted.

I am persuaded that the primary and most compelling reasons involve several economic considerations; certain natural conditions; family traditions; the importation of distilling techniques and equipment from European sources, largely during colonial days; personal preferences in drinking habits; the region's proximity to the legal distilling industry; a sympathetic community; an organization of law violators held over from Prohibition days; and a widespread belief that limestone water is essential to the production of good bourbon whiskey.

Historically, geographically, and statistically, Kentucky has fulfilled all of these conditions, and it is not accidental that from 1917 to 1957 the state was one of the major moonshine producing areas in the country. Economically, Kentucky has been dominated by a strong free enterprise philosophy that came into the region with settlers from Pennsylvania, Virginia, and the Carolinas. Moreover, the rugged terrain and poor soil of much of the state discouraged farming, although the rich bottomlands produced unlimited corn. The same landscape made transportation of liquor from the East into the area difficult and costly. Up to the present time in Kentucky, with the exception of areas where farms were large and prosperous, life could be hard and the living relatively meager, agricultural methods were comparatively primitive, and transportation over the hills was expensive. In a state that was not highly industrialized, jobs were few and cash was scarce. Therefore, moonshining could become a reliable source of income, and a concentrated moonshine operation can substitute for industry. Furthermore, moonshining requires no formal education or job references, and money from the traffic comes easy and fast.

In all communities where moonshining is common, there must be certain natural conditions that permit the making of illicit liquor. Primary among them are an adequate limestone water supply, preferably from a spring or group of springs; rugged, wooded terrain permitting adequate camouflage, and a population sparse enough to assure privacy. These conditions prevail along the headwaters of the literally thousands of streams that originate in the foothills or the mountains and flow into larger streams, leading to the Ohio, the Mississippi, and other major river systems. Much of the land here was fertile enough and the climate favorable enough to grow more corn than was needed for food and livestock. This was important in establishing whiskey making in earlier years; now these same moonshiners have shifted from corn to sugar, which is easily obtainable in wholesale lots. There is an abundance of cold limestone water from natural springs. The topography of the knob country and the mountains provides innumerable places where the location of small stills can be kept secret. And the sparse settlement characteristic of pioneer days remains so in comparison to other parts of the country.

Then, too, the tradition of moonshining runs in families. Through several generations, descendants of the immigrants who came from whiskey-producing areas in northern England, Scotland, and Ireland, and settled in the Appalachian area, have continued to make whiskey according to their old and revered family recipes. Occasionally, these families continue to produce moonshine whiskey, often in large quantities, even after they have increased their farming or business activities in a very substantial way, and have no pressing economic need. I have already alluded to the cases wherein one branch of the family will found and conduct a small legitimate distillery producing fine whiskey, while other branches of the same family continue to make moonshine.

Some areas of concentrated moonshine production in Kentucky are dotted with legal distilleries, many of them of considerable size. People here over a period of several generations have become well acquainted with methods of whiskey production, and some of them operate private stills in competition with their employers. It is understandable that the moonshiners of the central Kentucky area have the most efficient stills, more nearly resembling registered distilleries than those in other localities. The steam still, rather than the pot still, is universally used in this section. Certain big-time moonshiners of the Prohibition era, particularly in the Golden Pond area Between-the-Rivers (recently converted into a federal park between large and impounded Kentucky and Barkley lakes), used brand names based on the name of the individual moonshiner. One such brand was exploited throughout the Detroit, Dayton, and Cleveland areas. The demand grew to such proportions that the moonshiners resorted to buying other people's products to sell as their own, being too busy with marketing to bother with actual manufacture of the product.

Where organized moonshining exists, one of the foremost necessities is that the community be in sympathy with the traffic. For this reason, the incidence of moonshining varies from community to community within the same county, whether the county is wet or dry. In some communities, moonshining thrives because of tacit complicity on the part of the dominant religious group. In others, such considerations fail to suffice. I remember a conversation with an old-time moonshiner who was discussing the advisability of setting a still in a community where there was plenty of water during one very dry summer. "The main thing," he concluded, "is the people. Air they fur hit or air they agin hit?" Those who are "agin hit" are likely to report the activities to the officers and the resulting disruption of the enterprise might have far-reaching repercussions, such as fights, shootings, barn burnings, and much ill feeling among neighbors, not to mention the possibility that a few of the neighbors might get on probation from federal court or even spend a brief term in prison. However, in such areas, serving time does not bar the way to fiscal success. On the contrary, time served for liquor law violations enhances a man's opportunities for employment—up to a certain point. Thus, it is fair to say that there is always some sort of loose organization on a community basis, even though in any given town there may be only a few citizens involved; more often than not, however, a great many people in these communities actively participate.

In Kentucky the distribution of moonshining operations is largely determined by the relative location of "wet" and "dry" areas. Kentucky's local option law permits counties, and even precincts within counties, to license the legal sale of alcoholic beverages. It would seem reasonable for moonshining to flourish in dry areas, but this is not always the case. Dry counties may offer a better opportunity for bootlegging both legal whiskey and moonshine, but wet counties in Kentucky provide more of the demand as well as more of the illicit product.

Part of the explanation for this phenomenon may lie in the fact that many illegal dealers also own legal liquor stores and therefore hold federal licenses and have paid federal and state license fees. When such a dealer has paid his federal taxes he may be breaking local laws by selling in dry areas but he is not subject to federal prosecution, and penalties imposed by local courts tend to be slight. Hence, many moonshiners have purchased liquor stores and now furnish legal liquor to the bootleggers in dry territories. The same people operate in the same way, except that they are free from the harassment of federal officers and no longer manufacture the product they sell.

It is notable that in Kentucky many bootleggers are black, though whites are also well represented. It is rare, however, for blacks to enter the production end of the moonshine business and operate stills. This distinction does not hold in many of the states where moonshine is produced. But rural Kentuckians, for economic reasons, seem to tolerate a black bootlegger more readily than a black moonshiner.

Kentucky differs from states such as Tennessee and Georgia where tremendous markets for moonshine liquor exist in large cities. In places like Atlanta and Memphis, concentrations of unskilled labor and unemployed poor (many of them recently migrated from rural areas) swell the market for cheap moonshine. By contrast, Louisville, Kentucky, while it absorbs some of the moonshine produced in the state, does not have so large a market.

With respect to geographical distribution, we are concerned with three major areas in Kentucky and one, now largely of historical interest, immediately across the Tennessee River and the state line.

The first area consists of Nelson and Marion counties and some of the region immediately adjacent. Here numerous legitimate distilleries operate and moonshiners are quite conversant with the technology used in legitimate distilling. Most moonshiners in this area use a somewhat crude and much smaller replica of the steam still used in legal distilleries. These operators have a high rate of efficiency, for moonshiners. They produce a high daily yield, and during the 1950s 300 gallons per day was not unusual. Buying and selling are done in large quantities, and the wholesale phase of the business is well developed. Transportation is handled by skilled, fast drivers equipped with cars capable of performing superbly at very high speed. Some division of labor exists at the still, with one man holding the post of chief distiller and several others working as still hands. While the chief distiller may own the still, it is even more common for a third person or associated parties, known as *backers*, to own and finance operations. In the Nelson County area there is a higher degree of organization, some of it left over from Prohibition days, than is found elsewhere in the state. Operators there are more sophisticated in their knowledge of the market, their use of convenient political connections, and their investment of profits. Some have become very wealthy men.

Most of the whiskey produced in this two-county area is consumed locally or shipped within a radius of 100 or 150 miles. It is available in all towns and small cities of northern and central Kentucky.

The second moonshine area in Kentucky, Golden Pond, now called Land-Between-the-Lakes, cuts across the state near Kentucky Lake. This area, until recently very wild and sparsely inhabited, is crisscrossed by many deep creeks that drain into the Cumberland River. In many cases, the only access to stills was by boat, supplies being transported in and whiskey transported out on the water at night. Other stills could be reached by old logging trails over which a wagon or stone-boat could be driven. Throughout this area are pockets of sedimentary iron ore which were worked extensively in the mid-nineteenth century. Crude stone blast furnaces had been built, and the stone from these structures often served admirably as masonry foundations for large stills. Small towns in the vicinity, such as Cadiz and Princeton, served as collection and distribution points for whiskey in Prohibition days, bringing a high level of prosperity to this area. While stilling is rapidly dimin-

56

ishing in the large federal park area, it continues to flourish adjacent to the park on all sides. Here, the old-fashioned warning system of "two shoots" is still used, and there is an effective organization to warn of the approach of outsiders. Moonshiners here still retain their traditional copper pot stills, some of them very large. Often, bootleggers still sell moonshine from boats on the small creeks flowing into Barkley Lake and Kentucky Lake. On the Tennessee side of the Cumberland system, a short time ago, it was not unusual to find copper pot stills of one thousand-gallon capacity. Today, however, steam stills are also found in this area. Most of the production from this area in Prohibition days went to large cities in the North, especially to Detroit, and a considerable amount of it is still shipped outside the area.

In eastern Kentucky, the third major area, stills are much smaller (twenty- to fifty-gallon capacity). The equipment is primitive and the technology is traditional, steam stills rarely being found. One encounters makeshift equipment here, and it is not unusual to find moonshine made in a steel drum or in two steel drums welded together. Generally speaking, moonshiners here are predominantly older men who live on small farms and operate the still single-handed or with the help of a son or a neighbor's boy. Wood is the fuel of choice, the stills are set in the open, and the whiskey is usually stored underground in quart or half-gallon Mason jars. Wholesaling is not uncommon, for the moonshiner usually sells his product to the local bootlegger or to individual customers direct from his *stash*. While local whiskey runners sometimes transport small loads of whiskey from this area, most of it is consumed locally. The quality of whiskey in eastern Kentucky is often better than that encountered elsewhere, largely because more corn is used and some producers still age their whiskey. Occasionally one encounters small quantities of well-made corn whiskey aged in charred barrels and reminiscent of what really good old-time moonshine was like.

Just south of the Cumberland River and on the Tennessee line is a fourth area that, while small and only peripherally related to Kentucky, is of interest because of certain distinctive characteristics. This is known as Coe Ridge, a long hogback running for more than twenty miles along the state line. It is very rough terrain, once owned by a timber-producing family and later invaded by squatters, many of whom appear to be a mixture of Negroes, Indians, and Caucasians. Roads are almost nonexistent; small cabins are set in isolated clearings where there is little effort to raise crops or even to plant kitchen gardens. Small pot stills are used, the chief product being sugar whiskey laced with corn. Here survive customs that were once common in Virginia and the Carolinas—the distillation of brandy from apples, peaches, plums, and even wild fruits and berries. Large poplar fermentation vats are built in the open near the still and the source of spring water, and hand-operated presses remove the juices from the pummies. It is interesting that most of the production of this area is run out by transporters to central and northern Indiana. The quality of liquor produced here is inferior, and the people are isolated, hostile, suspicious, and shy. They tend to be threatening and even dangerous to outsiders. The character of this area is changing rapidly, however, and moonshining is disappearing. Many of the moonshiners seem to be following the path of their product and moving to Indianapolis and vicinity where for many years there was a strong demand for their liquor. However, Coe Ridge was never one of the major moonshine producing districts in the southeastern region.

Although the three areas discussed above have been the major whiskey-producing areas in the state, this does not mean that other areas do not have dedicated craftsmen pursuing a very old vocation. It is probable that in all sizable Kentucky communities (a few bone-dry towns excepted) there is at least one competent moonshiner who is either practicing the art or has practiced it in the past. It is not my intention to slight or overlook the endeavors of these artisans.

5

MONEY, MATERIALS, AND EQUIPMENT

A person who can't pay, gets another person who can't pay, to guarantee that he can pay.
CHARLES DICKENS, *Little Dorrit*

EVERY BUSINESS must be financed, and moonshining is no exception. In fact, even a small pot still may involve cash expenditures of $1,500 to $2,000 for equipment and initial operating expenses. A large steam still may mean an investment of $40,000 to $50,000. These amounts are necessary to purchase the still and auxiliary equipment and to start producing whiskey; afterwards, the daily running expenses must be met in cash, including the purchase of materials, the repair and maintenance of equipment, the use of cars and trucks, the payment of protection money (where this is the case), and the payment of wages to still hands. All these costs mount up, and the moonshiner must move his whiskey quickly after production in order to have the cash to continue operation.

Any break in the movement of whiskey from the still to the wholesaler or bootlegger is hazardous. The accumulation of a week's output without an immediate market can be disastrous. Once customers realize that a moonshiner is overstocked, they may begin dickering over the price, and the moonshiner will be forced either to take a price that cuts his profit, or even to incur a loss. In addition, the accumulation of large amounts of whiskey makes the moonshiner very vulnerable to a raid, since information about large stashes of whiskey tends to circulate rapidly. Sometimes these raids are precipitated by competitors who seize the opportunity to put the moonshiner out of business, eliminate large quantities of his product from the market, and secure for themselves the opportunity to take over that market.

Dealings with the law are very expensive, and moonshine cases are fought hard with the assistance of excellent legal talent. Even if the moonshiner is acquitted, he must have reserves at all times to meet these contingencies. If he is convicted, a situation involving imprisonment, fines, and expensive payments of back income tax, he must have even greater resources. All this means that he must either possess enough money or property to sustain him or be able to borrow funds in some quantity and have the collateral to guarantee such loans.

The small operator may have a copper pot still that he has had for years and needs only to be repaired or partially rebuilt each season. He purchases cornmeal and sugar at a general store where his credit may be good for thirty days or more. In order to operate a fifty-gallon still, he will need five one hundred-pound bags of sugar and one hundred and twenty pounds of cornmeal, provided he uses ten pounds of cornmeal to the barrel of mash. He will also need to purchase other equipment and materials. It will cost him from $100 to $200 a day just to operate.

Furthermore, it is difficult for one man to operate a still alone. If he hires a still hand, he will pay at least $30.00 a day in wages. He may solve this problem by taking in a partner who will share the cash expenditures and the labor in return for a share of the profits. Or he may, as many small-time isolated moonshiners do, draft one or two of his young sons to help him at the still, and do his own financing. If he does not have the ready cash for materials, he may get along on credit at the store, but this is dangerous because federal officers can examine the books. If he is an experienced and regular moonshiner, he is likely to have cash reserves or real estate against which he can borrow at the bank. However, he is always reluctant to borrow heavily against his own farm, since this represents his only security.

As we move up the scale into the area of larger producers, expenses mount very rapidly. A man who produces 300 gallons of moonshine a day may have expenditures of $300 a day for materials and perhaps another $100 a day in wages for two or three still hands. If we add another $50 a day for fuel and other incidental expenses, we see that he must sell enough whiskey each day to cover running expenses of approximately $450 before he can make any profit. And this data does not take into account the original cost of a large still. Moreover, the ordinary farm truck will hardly suffice for large operations, and the moonshiner will usually own at least one truck, one car, and numerous gasoline or electric motors which are used in production.

The large-scale moonshiner is usually a rather substantial citizen, with adequate cash and real estate to sustain him during the normal course of operation. On the other hand, he may be without extensive resources of his own, but because he is known for his skill, his discretion, and his ability to evade capture, he can interest a backer who will finance the entire project in return for a substantial share of the profits. These backers are people with considerable means and are often prominent citizens in the community. Often they will back several stills simultaneously, although they always maintain a very low profile in connection with moonshine activities. It is not unusual for such men to back reliable moonshiners over a period of many years with very favorable financial results.

Backers are usually very discreet about their activities

and choose the men they back with great care, basing their selection on the man's technical skill, his known reputation for integrity and reliability, and his family history as it relates to moonshine matters. Also, the backer often has potent political connections which he may use in a quiet way to protect operators whom he finances. On occasion, the backer may also finance transportation and marketing ventures when these are an integral part of the production scheme.

Although the moonshiner's profits are high, he uses high-risk capital to finance his ventures. Many moonshiners do not have sufficient financial stability to weather setbacks or temporary disasters. Therefore, the rate of financial failure is high among those who do not have their own resources or adequate outside backing.

Regardless of the size or type of still operated, the raw materials of moonshine are standard. The principal ingredient is, of course, sugar, which is bought and stockpiled in one hundred-pound bags. Sugar is ordered in quantity through one or more general stores where the proprietor is a discreet person who maintains the thin fiction that the purchaser's wife must be canning incredible quantities of fruits and berries. The sugar is picked up in truckload lots; temporary storage may be had in a barn or other building on the premises of the moonshiner, or may on occasion be held in the stockroom of the storekeeper until needed. Quantities sufficient for at least one day's setting of mash are hauled to the still site and stored under a large tarpaulin or under a light shed constructed for this purpose. The sugar is hauled from the barn to the still site in such a way as to leave as little traffic *sign* as possible. Eight or ten bags may be hauled in on a stone-boat or farm sled drawn by a single mule or a team. These sleds have wooden runners that pass easily over grass and soft earth, and their tracks do not draw attention because the sleds are commonly used for moving equipment, feed, firewood, and other materials around a farm. Sometimes the stone-boat is pulled by a tractor, whose tire marks are seen all over the farm, or by a *weed-monkey,* an old junker of a car often stripped of the body. Where gasoline or kerosene is used to power pumps or other equipment, this fuel is hauled in by the same means, though great care must be exercised to prevent contact between the sugar or cornmeal and the kerosene or gasoline, since a very small contamination can ruin an entire batch of whiskey. Where wood is used for fuel, one or more mules are kept at the still site in harness with a singletree dangling from the traces. These mules are used to haul poles from the woods as they are cut and trimmed for fuel. In fact, one or more mules are commonly found at the still site, where they are kept between trips and used as a power source for moving heavy objects.

In the operation of small stills, or where traffic by mule team or truck is not feasible, the raw materials may be carried in on the backs of men who make several trips after dark or before daylight in order to get the raw materials into place. Pack mules are also occasionally used, with each one carrying two or three one hundred-pound bags of sugar. In large-scale operations, traffic is very difficult to conceal since raw materials must be hauled in on trucks or in cars. Sometimes large consignments of sugar are brought in on a farm wagon hauled by a tractor. These materials must be moved cautiously to avoid attracting attention.

The cornmeal, which may constitute about one-tenth of the raw materials, is brought in and handled in the same way as the sugar. It is usually obtained at the same store that supplies the sugar, though it may be bought at a local mill or even ground from corn raised on the farm of the moonshiner.

In areas where fruit is fermented and distilled, large quantities must first be assembled at the still site. These may be purchased from neighboring farmers and trucked in or may be grown on the farm where the still is located. Fruit is distilled only during a very limited season, and a brandy still will operate only during a few weeks in the late summer. In some areas, the moonshine still is used to process the fermented fruit during the season and then returned to whiskey making; in other areas separate brandy stills, usually smaller than whiskey stills, are used for distilling fruit. In all brandy operations, large quantities of sugar are used in order to increase the alcohol content of the mash.

In addition to grain and possibly fruit, the moonshiner needs malt, a considerable quantity of flour to seal the cap on the still between *charges,* and commercial yeast, which is purchased at the local level. He will also need considerable amounts of lime for scrubbing and cleaning the fermentation vats or barrels between batches. Commercial lime is bought in sacks and kept under cover at the still site.

All these materials must be purchased and kept available so that a steady supply can be transferred to the still site each day without interruptions. Care is also taken to keep a minimum of materials at the site and to protect them carefully against rain and weather. Running out of any basic raw material can prove costly, since it means the entire operation must be temporarily discontinued.

Perhaps the most liberally used essential raw material is free—or nearly so. This is water, which is used for setting the mash, cooling the flakestand, and cleaning the still and the mash vats after each use. Because many spring-fed streams run only part of the year, smaller-scale moonshining tends to be seasonal and operates during those months of the year—late fall, winter, spring, and early summer—when water flows steadily and abundantly. Some moonshiners use municipal water supplies or have access to deep wells that supply water of uniform quality year-round. These operators can run throughout the dry months if they choose. But the use of municipal or commercial water supplies involves contact with nearby settlements, which constitutes a certain hazard to illicit whiskey making. Furthermore, the disposal of *spent mash* constitutes a real problem unless an adequate sewage system is available to absorb the odorous by-products without betraying the location of the still.

Fermenters, of course, are essential, no matter what type of still is being used. The simplest fermenter is an ordinary oak barrel. Its age and condition are unimportant so long as it will hold liquid. The source of these barrels is usually a legitimate distillery, which always has used barrels to sell, since the law requires that a barrel can be used only once to age bourbon. This law is not very logical, since whiskey can easily be aged in barrels that have been in use for many years. But the law is the law, and legitimate distillers must discard old barrels and substitute new ones for all bourbon that they produce and age.

Until about 1965 the used barrels could be purchased from small distilleries, which, in Kentucky, are often not far from moonshine areas. Today, however, new barrels are very expensive and used barrels are sold at a good figure for varying purposes, including the manufacture of furniture. Many barrels are dismantled, reconditioned, and shipped to industrial users abroad, especially in South America. Such a reconditioning plant now operates at Springfield, Kentucky.

For small moonshine stills, the barrels are set in batteries or decks with enough new mash started on consecutive days so that each day a new charge of still-beer is available for that day's run. Thus, a one hundred-gallon still charged twice a day would require 200 gallons of fresh still-beer for each day's run. Some moonshiners run only one charge per day, and others several, depending upon the help available, weather, speed of fermentation, and other factors. The barrels for fermentation are arranged very near the still and are so positioned that one deck of barrels theoretically contains the mash necessary for an entire day's run. A small still might require as few as twenty barrels. A large still might require a great many barrels—too many for convenient handling of the materials.

Large stills, therefore, are frequently fed by very large vats made of squared poplar timbers bolted together securely, and, like the barrels, often buried in the ground to assure optimal temperatures. Both the barrels and the vats must be emptied rapidly when still-beer is needed. For small pot stills, the beer is dipped from the barrels by bucket and poured into the still. In large operations, the dipping process would be quite inefficient, so power pumps are frequently used to convey the beer through long, heavy, flexible hoses from the vats to the still. The pumps used for this purpose are usually gasoline-powered, although in some areas electricity may be used. The motors, which are usually of about ½ horsepower, run only when beer is being transferred from the still, or when water is being pumped from the creek, spring, or other water source in order to set new mash or to cleanse the vats. These pumps constitute a certain hazard to the moonshiner since their engines make a characteristic noise that can be heard for a long distance.

After each use, the fermenters must be fully cleansed with clean water under pressure supplied through a flexible hose. The same, of course, is true of the still and its auxiliary equipment, which are thoroughly cleaned between runs.

The poplar vats are made of heavy timbers, usually 4 x 6, 4 x 8, or 4 x 10, which are produced at local sawmills. At each still site one usually finds a considerable supply of rough-cut lumber used to build and repair vats and to construct the *mash-floor* around the still where the men work. This floor is supported by rough field-stone pillars or by short upright piling. Sometimes the floor is nailed to slender tree trunks felled across the stream and trimmed. The floor itself is built high enough above the ground (sometimes actually over the creek) to keep the men out of the accumulating decayed mash that characterizes outdoor distilling. At large stills, these floors can be hosed down regularly and are heavy enough to support the handling of heavy equipment, or even the cars and trucks which on rare occasion are driven to and from the still. Rough timber is also used in the construction of the shed that shelters supplies at the larger stills. Often these sheds are made from posts cut in the immediate vicinity and used as uprights between which the scantlings are nailed, and over which rough sheeting is applied to keep out the rain. The tops of these sheds are often covered with evergreen cedar boughs or other brush as a crude form of camouflage.

At every still, there is a keg or chest or half-barrel filled with crude tools and a supply of heavy nails, spikes, bolts, and the like, used for maintenance of equipment. There is also a saw—perhaps a heavy cross-cut saw—one or more axes, shovels, a mattock, and other trenching tools used to clear the brush and direct or control the flow of water. There are usually one or more large tarpaulins used to cover the fermenters and perhaps the supplies if they are not fully protected in the shed.

Then, of course, there are the stills themselves. Steam stills tend to involve more money and necessary equipment than do pot stills. Although pot stills do vary in size, the large steam stills are very much larger than the largest pot stills. Small ones may have an ordinary steel drum for a boiler and a small aluminum or copper tank or indeed a large oaken hogshead for a cooker. Large steam stills may use commercial steam boilers or the boilers of railroad locomotives cut down to the desired capacity. The cookers may be proportionately large and made either of metal or, more frequently, of silo staves held together in a tight cylinder by heavy turnbuckles. These wooden still units may have a capacity of 1,000 gallons or more, but as the capacity of the cooker goes up, provisions must be made for a steady supply of preheated beer in order to maintain production. A steam still with a one thousand-gallon cooker capacity will require a very large backlog of fermenter vats run in cycles so that large amounts of finished still-beer are available daily to keep the operation running smoothly. The problem of disposal of slops is always acute for a big still, though the same problem exists with small stills as well. Big stills cannot simply run the slops through a trough in the hogpen or flush them into an adjacent stream. Mash, beer, and slops are shifted by hand in the small steam stills as in the pot stills, but with the bigger steam stills power pumps are essential to transfer the large amounts of beer produced, to cleanse the mash vats, to provide hot slops for the scalding of new mash, and to provide fresh water for the boiler and fermenters.

It is not uncommon to encounter steam stills producing 300 gallons of whiskey a day, and there are a few that can produce upwards of 1,000 gallons a day. Yet these are not nearly so large as the great alky columns that one finds in New York and Chicago, which do not exist in Kentucky. In fact, the Kentucky phase of moonshining is not geared to the marketing and distribution of anything over about 300 gallons a day, since the market will not absorb large quantities and the moonshiner cannot afford to store whiskey in which large amounts of money are tied up.

In addition to the still's proper and auxiliary equipment, the moonshiner must have available numerous spare parts and tools for the installation and operation of a still. He must have these either at the still site or nearby in his or someone else's barn. He needs copper plate for patching and repairs, copper pipe for replacement when necessary, and some quantity of rough-cut lumber for building mash vats and other construction work. There will also be a considerable array of plumber's tools such as pipe wrenches, cutters, threaders, soldering equipment, and so forth; for a large steam still requires the services of an experienced steamfitter. Axes and shovels are also essential to the operation. Trucks are a necessity for a large steam still, and access to roads must be made and used at the risk of betraying the location of the still.

Also, containers of various kinds are legion at the site. At the pot still large numbers of barrels are often required for use as fermenters, and around any kind of still extra barrels are much in demand and always in evidence. Frequently they need minor repairs, which are made on the spot. The containers for whiskey must be provided in advance in standardized sizes and selected for various means of transportation. In mountain areas or around pot stills, the favored container is the Mason fruit jar in half-gallon size, though quarts may be encountered. They are usually kept in their original cardboard cases and are transported six or twelve to a case from the still. Individual mountain moonshiners who sell direct to the customer often bury these fruit jars in a thicket near the house and produce them one at a time as needed. It is often jokingly said in mountain moonshine country that all customers carry a permanent crease in the bridge of the nose as a result of drinking from a Mason jar. Where larger production is involved, the gallon cola jug in cases of four is the favorite. These cases are easy to handle, easy to pack in a car or truck, do not rattle, and up to a point, resist breakage. In the mountain areas a few old-fashioned *jacket-cans* are also still in use. These are cylindrical cans of five-gallon capacity encased in a thin veneer of wood and bound with wire hoops. During the 1950s when much military gear was sold as surplus, the five-gallon jerry or G.I. can, used to transport gasoline for military purposes, was much in demand, and many moonshiners acquired a stock of them which is still in use. These are ideal in many ways, since they save space in packing, do not break, and are constructed for easy and rapid handling. A big operation must have immediately available more than enough containers to put up each day's production and ready it for storage or distribution. These containers are hidden away in the brush or stacked under tarpaulins in the temporary shed that houses materials.

While for the very small one-man pot still this equipment and these materials can be easily assembled over a period of time preceding each run, for the larger steam still all these activities must be synchronized in such a way that each run blends smoothly into the next. And this requires organization which, though loose, parallels that which we find in legitimate industry.

6

MOONSHINING AS AN INDUSTRY

Delays have dangerous ends.
SHAKESPEARE, *Henry VI*

WITH THE ADVENT of Prohibition in 1919, moonshining took on some of the trappings of big business. Since the owner, part owner, or backer was now heavily preoccupied with sales, distribution, protection, and other such details, he needed a small hierarchy of people working under him to handle production. His contacts were primarily with large customers, sources of protection, and other moonshiners, all of which took him away from the still frequently. For these reasons moonshining became loosely organized as a business.

Capitalization: As in all businesses, financing is basic, and while the old-time one-man still required little investment, modern producers must have access to considerable amounts of ready cash and sufficient reserves to tide them over emergencies.

Any still large enough to require a backer will involve a potential investment of $3,000 to $5,000. And this still will be of small capacity. Some of the big steam stills in the Carolinas have a production capacity of 1,000 to 1,800 gallons per day and are very costly to build and operate. One raided near the Kentucky–Tennessee border in the spring of 1973 was reported by federal agents to have a mashing capacity of 15,000 gallons with a net daily yield of 1,500 to 2,000 gallons of 100 proof sugar whiskey. The initial cost of constructing this still was said to be some $40,000. Operating expenses were very high and the cost of marketing and transporting this volume of whiskey would be enormous. Sales and transportation would have to be expanded over a large area to find a market that could absorb 2,000 gallons of whiskey a day. In other words, within easy transporting distance, bootleggers would have to market some 16,000 pints of whiskey per day just to keep this still running. And of course, we must remember that there are competing stills in the same area. Obviously, the moonshine whiskey industry makes demands on capital that are not common in most legitimate industries.

It is practically unknown for backers to be prosecuted or convicted in connection with moonshining although it sometimes happens in connection with very large alky columns in big cities. The backer, needless to say, never associates himself publicly with any phase of the industry, though it is not unknown for a backer to own a legal liquor store that sells both moonshine and legal whiskey. In fact, there is an obvious trend for some backers to control outlets, handling more legal whiskey than moonshine whiskey, and a few deal exclusively in legal whiskey imported into dry areas where any whiskey is illegal.

Industrial Personnel: The still operator himself is a man of some experience and has the necessary connections to buy raw materials and sell whiskey. He probably comes from a family in which his father and grandfather were still operators. While he is well versed in distilling methods, he is basically a businessman. If the still is over one hundred-gallon capacity, there may be a chief stiller—that is, a still hand with a rather competent knowledge of equipment and technology; he can usually build, repair, or rebuild any still at which he works. Very often he has been employed previously in a

73

legitimate distillery; this is especially true where steam stills are involved. His rate of pay will be a little higher than an ordinary still hand's and he may have certain limited administrative authority.

On each still site there will be from two to four or five still hands, usually small farmers, who do the heavy work involved in production. Any or all of these men may have some technological competence and be experienced in moonshining. They are paid by the day at the going rate of $25.00 to $35.00 or more per day. These men work with the understanding that in the event of a raid they will "take the rap" for the owners, who will pay their fines, and they will serve time in prison if necessary without implicating the owner, unless he is caught red-handed. In a good organization, their families will receive some support. These are the men who are commonly seen in federal court when a moonshine case is being tried.

It is notable that few women are active in the distilling end of the illicit traffic. However, in rare instances women do own or operate or direct the operations of stills, and sometimes a woman is found at the still, usually serving as a *lookout*. Also, in rural areas, women may operate a small, usually *coffin*-type still on the kitchen stove, producing a gallon or so per day. This custom was more prevalent formerly than it is today. Overall, participation of women is minimal. However, while women are undoubtedly discriminated against in the distilling end of the business, they are commonly found as bootleggers and are sometimes quite successful financially. In some areas of the state women come to the still-site after a large and successful run and hold a celebration with their men; chickens and sweet corn are baked in the still furnace and a picnic lunch spread on the ground. Only when these festivities are held does whiskey drinking occur at the still, and during these times the still does not operate. The limited participation of women is perhaps explained partially by

74

the fact that work at the still is rough and even dangerous. But there is also the pervasive belief, perhaps influenced by taboo, that in the traditional division of labor men are responsible for the production of whiskey.

Industrial Security: The security of the still is protected by two types of employees. The first is a lookout, usually armed with a shotgun for signalling purposes, who remains hidden some distance from the still to warn of any approaching strangers. Usually he is an elderly man or a young teenager. The other type is a *guard* who is also armed but expected to put up a fight or at least delay officers attempting a raid. Their effectiveness exists primarily in the mind of any owner who believes they will protect him. Both guards and lookouts are paid varying wages according to their effectiveness, but sometimes lookouts are not paid at all because they are members of the owner's family.

Traffic and Transportation: The distribution of moonshine whiskey is usually independent of its production. Likewise, the men who handle transportation are very different from those who produce the whiskey. The transporters are usually very young men, expert drivers who have neither the knowledge nor the desire to run a still. While whiskey is transported in all kinds of vehicles, from trucks to boats, the ordinary passenger sedan seems to be the favorite. Today these cars are available in high-speed models made by various manufacturers as part of the conventional line. They are purchased by officers and transporters alike and easily outperform the very best of the souped-up cars used by both in the period from 1945 to 1965.

In those days, when the federals had no money for purchasing hot cars, the transporter had the work done at high cost while the officers hoped to confiscate enough such cars to engage in effective pursuit. In subsequent years, all this has changed, but a few of the old-time souped-up models are still in service in some areas. Today they are called "junkers" and are regarded as the type of transportation that can be abandoned by the driver if pressed, left to crash beside the road, or meander driverless down the highway, thereby perhaps delaying pursuit.

These cars were prepared by expert mechanics and machinists who knew that they were servicing transporters, and charged accordingly. Certain makes and models were preferable in certain areas, and the car usually had a nondescript appearance that was deceptive. Underneath the hood it was a different story, for the chrome-plated engine was souped-up to outdistance any conventional factory model. Often three carburetors were lined up on the engine head, the last one delivering raw gas at speeds over 100 miles per hour. Gear ratios were modified, and an extra battery replaced the generator in order to send the entire horsepower of the engine to the drive shaft. This power in turn was increased phenomenally by expanding the cylinder bore and installing oversized pistons. The back seats were removed or removable so that the trunk and the back seat became a continuous compartment capable of holding up to 100 gallons of whiskey. The front seats were welded in and oversized tires were desirable. Usually oversized shock absorbers or load lifters were installed over the rear axle to prevent the car from riding low when loaded. These cars were notoriously hard to start. They sputtered and limped along in urban traffic, but once on the open road their performance at high speed was amazing.

Every small town in a liquor producing area has one or more young transporters around the age of twenty who tend toward a prototype. In some regions they constitute a definite social caste, having a high income, great local status, and strong interests in making money, pursuing girls, and gambling. Their dress tends to be casually expensive and very much more sporty than that of local citizens. Their almost neurotic attachment to the automobile, coupled with their preoccupation with speed and their superb driving, often leads them to stock-car races. A few of them graduate to big-time racing. The concepts of power and speed are dominant in the thinking of these young men who have created for themselves a most romantic self-image. As soon as their reflexes slow down and caution influences their driving, they are no longer useful.

Transporters are paid from $1.00 to $2.00 per gallon according to the area, the risks involved, the quantity transported, and other factors. Usually the owner of the still makes arrangements for the transportation and pays the driver, the cost being passed on to the purchaser. In some areas the bootlegger hires and pays the transporter himself. These drivers spend as little time as possible around the still and do not openly associate with moonshiners. They are almost always unmarried, but often temporarily live with one of the less conventional girls in their own or a neighboring community. Their prowess with women is well known and their tastes run to the flashier type of girl. Since they are paid by the gallon, any risks they take are usually their own, and they may do time if caught. A considerable number are killed or maimed in high-speed chases and most of them at one time or another have been involved in a serious accident. When they no longer drive the hot transport cars, they tend to degenerate into a kind of soft and slovenly indolence, existing as best they can on the empty memories of their younger days.

Distribution: In areas where there is heavy production by large stills, we sometimes find a wholesaler or distributor who is a middleman between the moonshiner and the bootlegger. This man buys whiskey in quantity and sells it directly to the bootlegger. He must have considerable ready capital as well as a large area within which to operate. He makes his money on speculation, buying heavily when moonshiners are overstocked, balancing out the supply and demand, and selling for the highest price he can obtain. Sometimes a distributor may own or operate a still of his own on the side. These wholesalers are not as common in the moonshine areas of Kentucky as they are in Alabama, Tennessee, and the Carolinas.

Communications: All those who work with moonshining have a discreet, reliable, and sometimes quite complex system of communication. Transporters, wholesalers, and still operators have a particular need for this. Methods vary from county to county and details cannot be given here. However, there are three main sources through which law violators are alerted to the presence of danger. These are local telephone operators, rural mailmen, and local police or sheriff's deputies who may have a fiscal interest in protecting hometown moonshiners. In addition there are countless other individuals who are only too willing to "take the word" when suspicious strangers appear in the vicinity. In farming country children often perform this duty very effectively by running on foot through shortcuts known only to them.

Industrial Hazards: The moonshining industry employs machinery, some of it quite dangerous, and, as is the case in any industry, accidents will happen. Still hands, however, are not protected by industrial insurance or hospitalization, and while the still owners tend to cover the cost of small accidents, major mishaps can remove a man permanently from the labor market. When stills operate under a heavy head of steam, they can and often do explode, usually as the result of careless handling of the fire. The homemade boilers of steam stills are also hazardous, and most moonshiners have at one time or another been scalded by live steam escaping from a cap or a leaking pipe. In the course of handling the tools and power equipment connected with steam stills, injuries are not uncommon. Chain saws, axes, compressors, motor-driven belts, and the like are as hazardous there as in any legitimate industry.

Haulers of supplies and transporters are particularly vulnerable to traffic accidents.

More exotic types of mishaps occur that do not ordinarily affect industrial workers. These include injury from firearms discharged intentionally, accidentally, or playfully at the still site. Unreliable employees may also become intoxicated on fresh whiskey or even still-beer and fall into the fire or into the vats when overcome by carbon dioxide. All moonshiners must suffer from varying degrees of damage from drinking their own product, and chronic alcoholism is not uncommon. Certainly living and working in the environment of the still affords the worker few of the benefits known to the workers of a business with safety and sanitation programs. There are no union stewards to carry grievances to management or arbitration boards.

Quality Control: Perhaps the less said about this subject the better. However, old-time moonshine whiskey has about it a romantic aura that was once undoubtedly deserved. Today the ordinary run of commercial moonshine whiskey has only two criteria for quality control. The first is the way it holds a bead in the temping bottle. The second is a casual taste test provided by occasionally sampling the whiskey from the catch-can. If it holds a bead and no fatalities arise from the taste test, it is considered ready for the market. This lack of quality control is undoubtedly one of the reasons why the business is declining. The old-timers who acquired a taste for illicit liquor during Prohibition days are now reduced in numbers and a younger generation of drinkers is not willing to undergo the rigorous training program necessary to drink and retain moonshine.

Taxation: Most businesses have tax problems. The moonshiner, however, either has no tax problem at all or tax problems so complex and devastating that they can wipe him out and put him in prison. It is interesting to note that the moonshiner is one of the few industrialists who adhere closely to the true spirit of free enterprise. While almost every other industry receives some subsidy from the government, the moonshiner rejects subsidies along with taxes, which he regards as immoral. To him, fermentation of grain and distilling are natural, God-given processes, and no government has the right to tax them. He has held this position since colonial days and still maintains it stubbornly. His attitude toward state and local taxes is identical, though he seldom worries much about these. The real threat comes from the federal government. If caught and convicted, he can be charged back taxes on an estimated production from his still as well as penalties and back payments, or given a prison sentence involving non-payment of income tax. Therefore he sticks to his free enterprise philosophy with considerable daring, not a little courage, and a tenacity that would have delighted Adam Smith and the colonial practitioners of laissez faire. It is not accidental that Massachusetts, the cradle of independence, was also the cradle of the illicit liquor industry, the town of Bedford in 1776 supporting over seventy-five rum distilleries. Our history books do not emphasize the fact that when Paul Revere cried, "The British are coming," he was referring to the collectors of British revenue tax—their number somewhat diminished since the revenue ship *Gaspé* had been burned in Boston harbor.

At the same time, the evasion of taxes is the only factor that enables the moonshiner to stay in business at all. In effect—though he would deny it—he operates under a benign subsidy of $10.50 or more a gallon.

Rationale: The moonshiner is always handicapped by his failure to integrate production with sales, and this lack of integration has increased geometrically as stills have grown larger and production has increased. The legitimate distiller gets weekly or even daily reports from salesmen who supply the wholesale market. As so many hundreds of cases of legal whiskey are sold, or their sale anticipated, a sufficient number of barrels of aged whiskey is removed from bond in the warehouse and bottled to replace it. In the production division itself, production is geared to replace in the warehouse a given number of barrels to be put under bond and aged for ultimate sale four or more years later. Thus the distillery must have reserves of aging whiskey worth millions of dollars, and the industry is so geared that demands can be filled, reserves replenished, and production continued at a reasonably stable level. The moonshine industry has no such organization. If the still owner has an order for 50 or 100 gallons it is usually to be delivered on short notice and often warm from the still. Since bootleggers are his chief customers he does not know at what time arrests or raids may put a number of them out of business. Therefore, the moonshiner is always a marginal producer and cannot expand beyond a limited point and survive the uncertain economics of his own industry. This along with the deteriorating quality of the whiskey accounts for the noticeable decline in moonshine production in the last few years.

LAW ENFORCEMENT

*'Tis my vocation, Hal; 'tis no sin
for a man to labor in his vocation.*
SHAKESPEARE, *Henry IV, Part I*

SINCE THE WHISKEY Rebellion in 1791–1792, the chief thorn in the side of the moonshiner has been the federal agent who collects the liquor tax. Originally these agents rode horseback over wide areas, visited anyone manufacturing whiskey, rum, or brandy, measured the capacity of the still, copied production figures from the stiller's journals, or even accepted the stiller's estimate of annual production. The revenue agent then was primarily concerned with collecting the tax and turning it over to the federal government, usually in the form of gold or silver coin. Only incidentally was the agent concerned with the suppression of unlicensed stills, though of course there were many. With taxes low and the price of whiskey low, the market could be supplied at a very reasonable price and at a profit for the farmer, the stiller, and the grocery-man who sold it by the bottle or jug, or the tavern keeper who sold it by the drink.

It must be remembered, however, that the resistance to licensing and taxation among stillers was strong from the start, and this resistance could not have been overcome by any staff of federal agents had they been inclined to attempt control. Once the principle of taxation was accepted, the legitimate distillers paid the small tax and the rebels refused, but there were still too few agents to assure adequate enforcement. Taxes went up until after the War of 1812, during which time more moonshining developed, for with higher taxes the moonshiner who did not pay them naturally had an advantage over the legitimate distiller who did. The years from 1817 to 1861 were a remarkable period that saw all federal taxes removed from whiskey. While the moonshiner was free to operate, it was difficult for him to compete against well-organized and regularly operating established stills, which often ran in conjunction with a consistently productive water mill. It was during this period that Kentucky acquired the beginnings of its reputation for producing excellent whiskey. This reputation perhaps originated among the relatively few travelers who sampled whiskey in Kentucky, but the reputation was enhanced far more by the large quantities of corn whiskey exported from the state, especially in the riverboat trade. Flatboats on the Ohio, the Salt River, the Kentucky River, the Green River, the Barren River, and the mighty Cumberland and all its branches not only helped Kentucky farmers and millers to prosper but also made Kentucky "likker" famous from New Orleans to Pittsburgh.

Economically the small state liquor tax levied by Kentucky gave the state a favorable marketing position in comparison to states where taxes were higher and the quality of the product was not so good. Meanwhile, records show not a single visit by federal revenuers to any of the stillers in Kentucky, and this propitious situation lasted until the Civil War, when high federal taxes were imposed and federal revenue men again appeared. From this time on the Kentucky moonshiner was never free from the threat of federal arrest, especially during the days of Prohibition, when Kentucky enjoyed national fame as the producer of good quality illicit whiskey.

At this point we should perhaps mention that state enforcement policies, derived originally from Virginia's, have been in existence intermittently down to the present time but have never been enforced with the vigor and effectiveness of federal laws, nor have the penalties for violations of state tax been so severe.

Federal agents have always been relatively few in number. In the past twenty years, however, better coverage has been provided Kentucky, and today approximately forty agents operate regularly in the state. These men must cover a very wide range of rough terrain, much of which is wooded and not easily accessible to motor vehicles. Parenthetically, they also have many auxiliary duties in connection with tax matters, tobacco control, and the enforcement of the federal firearms laws. In the late nineteenth and early twentieth centuries these men were a truly heroic breed, for open warfare existed between them and the moonshiners, and many a revenue agent was "buried on the point," that is, he was shot from ambush, dragged to a sharp ridge separating hollows, then covered with a felled cedar tree and left to the buzzards. The point of the ridge was chosen since hunters or travelers would be most likely to follow the creekbed and not the ridge. Before Prohibition days revenue agents traveled on horseback, afoot, or by boat. They covered very large territories at irregular intervals and were engaged not only in collecting tax but also in suppressing moonshining where this could be done. Kentuckians isolated in the backwoods attained an especially strong feeling of independence and freedom from oppression by the law, together with a high reputation in personal combat with fists, Bowie knives, or forearms. Federal agents therefore had to be strong men capable of meeting moonshiners on their own grounds and highly dedicated to the work in which they specialized. Like federal marshals in the old West, they were often sustained by a love of combat and almost unlimited reserves of controlled violence. Pitched battles with moonshiners were not uncommon in those days. Of course, officers of this caliber were few, the territory large, their work arduous, and the percentage of moonshine stills taken undoubtedly small, but they kept alive a very real threat of the federal law.

During Prohibition days business boomed for the moonshiners, and the car, the truck, and the motorboat entered into the bigtime traffic where roads and rivers permitted. The revenue men also had wheels, and the chases that we know today began to develop on the back roads of Kentucky. At this time, a new and different type of federal officer entered the picture. Replacing the strong, level-headed, courageous frontier lawmen represented by the federal revenue agents, came a horde of undisciplined, untrained, unprincipled men known as "Prohibition agents." They created havoc in the state by using all forms of harassment, entrapment, and abuse to make arrests and secure convictions. Their record is not a pretty one in any state but it was particularly vivid in Kentucky because of the amount and quality of whiskey being exported for a national market.

Following Prohibition the legitimate distilling industry became strongly organized and began to produce high-quality whiskey. The interests of the government were looked after by resident revenue agents, known as whiskey gaugers, who stayed on the premises of each distilling company. These men did not chase moonshiners but carried out the rather exacting bookwork necessary to calculate taxes due on whiskey production. They also supervised installation of stilling equipment to meet federal regulations, estimated evaporation allowances in warehouses, and credited distilleries with losses of whiskey that could not be taxed under the law. These gaugers still operate at each Kentucky distillery, but are not primarily interested in moonshiners, though they may occasionally pass on information based on hearsay. They are usually concerned with enforcing the laws governing production and warehousing, and especially with violations committed either by management or by employees involving the surreptitious removal of untaxpaid liquor, sometimes in large quantities. Their presence is now accepted equitably by legitimate distillers, whose relations with the Internal Revenue Service are generally good. After all, they protect the profits of the legal industry.

Meanwhile, in reaction to the bad reputation cultivated by the so-called Prohibition agents, the Internal Revenue Service developed a new breed of officer whose main concern was field work. These men gradually developed into a very effective law enforcement unit. They were well-trained in law enforcement techniques, had good liaison with other federal agencies, and tried to develop insofar as was possible cordial relations with state and local officers in the districts where they worked. They were well trained in self-defense, expert with firearms, and very capable of driving at the highest speeds necessary to catch whiskey transporters.

Today, such officers are usually natives of the state and often of the area in which they work, which gives them a great advantage in developing rapport with the rural and small town populace. Some of the older revenue men are skilled woodsmen who can track a man through the woods or across fields running at full speed. They have incredibly sharp eyes for footprints in the dust or in soft earth and a highly developed capacity for reading dusty tire tracks carried from a side road onto a blacktop surface.

But whatever other skills the agent may have, he will not be very successful unless he knows how to locate and recruit stool pigeons—people willing to inform, often for pay—and to exploit effectively any information thus gained. It is an old saying that a little bit of specific information is worth a world of scientific training.

And no stranger can move into rural Kentucky and collect information on his own.

Informers come in all types, sizes, and shapes. Some people seem to be born informers, happily passing on whatever information they have about someone, whether that information is of value or not. Sometimes, however, these busybodies do have valid information. An agent must know how to sift the wheat from the chaff. What is more, though these people seldom provide the kind of specific and detailed information necessary to make a raid or catch a transporter, they are well known in the community as gossips and it is convenient sometimes to use them as a cover for more discreet and effective informers. The eager informants, meanwhile, may be either male or female, women playing more of a part than some might suspect. Sometimes given information can be quite lethal, as in the case of a woman who is having an affair with a moonshiner or transporter, finds herself jilted, but continues to receive crucial information, which she passes on to officers. She usually does this anonymously if possible, by letter, by phone call, or by simply dropping the information where she knows it will be conveyed by others.

Of course, not all informers are naive or vengeful gossips. Nor do all female informers have a romantic contact with the racket. Often they are simply farm women who disapprove of moonshining and learn that a still has surreptitiously been located on their property. They do not consider themselves informers but merely dutiful citizens protecting their own property and reputation. In recent years old customs have changed to the extent that one moonshiner, usually a big operator, will pass on reliable information about a competitor, who is also likely to be a big producer. If this information is reliable and the officers act accordingly, moonshiner Number One may remove moonshiner Number Two from competition and acquire his market. This type of informing

87

is a rather recent development and violates all the canons of ethics previously existing in the craft. This activity, moreover, can be very dangerous and requires the utmost discretion on the part of both the informer and the federal officers, who have a kind of tacit obligation to protect the source of their information.

Perhaps the most commonly used informer is a law violator who has been arrested and arraigned but not yet tried for moonshining or transporting liquor. This man is naturally worried about his future, especially if he knows that there is a good case against him. In some instances he may assume or be led to believe that he can expect more lenient treatment in court if he cooperates with the officers, who imply or promise that they will report his cooperation to the prosecutor or even to the judge. These men often have intimate knowledge of the location of other stills, the delivery schedules of other transporters, or the whereabouts of fugitives who are wanted by the law. While "making deals" in connection with federal cases is often frowned upon officially, it is a fact that deals are often used to simplify the work of the prosecutor or to assist in the solution of other cases.

Of course, the information that such violators have is only good for a limited time, because soon after they are arraigned their contacts become less frequent and their knowledge less contemporary. And giving this kind of information away can be hazardous. In the old days it was almost sure death for the informer if his betrayal became known. Today stool pigeons seem to thrive better and live longer. However, no man whose complicity is known can live at ease in the community where he informed, even years after he assisted the officers to capture a friend or neighbor or even an enemy. Sometimes the informer is only cut up with a knife, beaten up, or marked in some way so that others will recognize him for an informant. In rare instances he may be tortured, as was a man in central Kentucky who was dragged in chains behind a car over a gravel road and left for dead.

He was permanently crippled and disfigured. Female informants are usually dealt with—sometimes violently—by their menfolk.

Another type of informer is the government employee who works his way into the confidence of producers or transporters and then calls in the officers. He is sometimes called an undercover man and is most effective when he makes large purchases of moonshine from a large producer or wholesaler. These purchases are made with marked money and frequently immediately precede a raid. Undercover men are feared and hated by moonshiners but are seldom killed since they have a quasi-official status as federal employees. They move from one part of the country to another and are quite skilled at convincing skeptical moonshiners that they should sell 50 or 100 gallons of whiskey to a total stranger.

While we are discussing informers we should perhaps mention what is known as the "dry snitch." This is incriminating information dropped in a casual and innocent manner into conversation with an officer with the information so phrased that although the officer is aware of the content, he cannot truthfully say that he was given specific information. This kind of snitch can come from any source, but often it is transmitted by local sheriffs or policemen who for one reason or another wish to eliminate a certain moonshiner but do not dare to make a raid or open arrest.

While these techniques do not reflect the traditional code of honor reported to be present among mountain people and especially among mountain moonshiners, they are essential to law enforcement and are quietly and effectively used by both the officers and the law violators. Incidentally, the ability to handle firearms often commands the respect of people in a moonshine community. It is interesting to note that while the moonshiners' weapon is the rifle, most agents are very well trained in the use of side arms, and the impression agents make with fast and accurate pistol fire is a favorable one for the law. This is underlined by the fact that while most moonshiners own and sometimes carry pistols, they are not usually expert in their use. Since Prohibition, the element of violence has gradually declined in law enforcement and resulted in a great reduction in the number of officers and moonshiners killed or wounded during raids.

One of the moonshiners' chief weapons in defense against law enforcement is camouflage. Thus the still site has to be selected to take advantage of all the natural and some artificial means of concealment. The rural moonshiner is expert at selecting a site that not only has the requisite water and wood for fuel but also the natural protection of woods and the kind of terrain that makes concealment easy and gives him a wide view of the approaches to the site. The site may be further obscured by partially covering it with a temporary roof of cedar boughs, and sometimes young cedars are sawed off at the base and placed in post holes to cover vulnerable areas. At night, some moonshiners surround the still with a spool of black cotton thread stretched from a flexible bush to keep it tight; before the moonshiner enters at dawn he pulls the end of the string, and if it is unbroken he knows that no one has entered the site. Some moonshiners sweep the path or earth about the still with a brush broom before they leave so that any footprints made during the night will be visible. The moonshiner has a very keen eye for tracking; he will spot a strange heelprint immediately. Where wood is used for fuel the moonshiner cuts ash poles with the slant of the stump always facing the hillside so that the sun does not pick up the bright reflection of the fresh-cut white wood, which can be seen for a half mile or more. In fact, the use of ash wood in itself is a subtle form of camouflage since it makes less smoke than any other native wood except dead chestnut. Where possible the stills are located in thick cover, frequently so carefully disguised that one may walk within a few yards of the still site without being aware of it. Occasionally one finds a still located in an open pasture through which there runs a creek with high banks. The still will be built on a crude platform over the creek, so constructed that no part of it appears above the creek bank. In a large pasture with grazing cattle, this kind of location can be secure, largely because no one would suspect the location of a still at that point. Also, the creekbed makes a convenient, concealed passageway over which supplies can be hauled by mules or even by tractor. Occasionally stills are located in caves that have an overhead air vent for the passage of smoke, or in abandoned coal mines that have convenient air shafts emerging on the hill behind the mine entrance. Where water floods the forward portion of the mine to a depth of three to four feet, the protection is doubled. While there is a popular belief that moonshine whiskey is made at night, this is true only in rare cases where the still is located within a cave, mine, or even a tobacco barn, so that the fire is not visible from the outside. A favorable location in the Kentucky hill country is the limestone overhang that one finds along the sides of the hollow, at the head of which a spring emerges. These limestone overhangs provide protection from the weather and a high degree of visual concealment, and are very helpful in reducing the noise that naturally emanates from a stilling operation.

Sometimes the still is further shielded by locating it away from the direct source of water but using a covered pipeline from the spring or stream to the still some distance away. Thus anyone following the hollow would not find the still unless he were fortunate enough to discover the carefully hidden intake pipe.

Federal agents must be able to cope with the elaborate system of concealment and camouflage that the moonshiner has to protect him. Hard work, much of it done in wooded areas infested by ticks, copperheads, mosquitoes, and other pests, along with a good knowledge of woodcraft and guerrilla tactics, is necessary for agents who intend to succeed in the field. Long years of experience have taught the old-time revenuers most of the tricks that the moonshiners know. They know how to stalk their prey skillfully, sometimes over several days and nights, how to locate the still despite clever screening, and when to raid it in order to get illicit whiskey and as many of the men who are making it as possible.

It is unusual to catch all the men who work at a still since at the first sign of a raid they melt into the woods with astonishing effectiveness. Sometimes fights erupt at the still if moonshiners show resistance, but usually no one is seriously hurt; after tempers cool the moonshiners frequently help the federal officers cut up the still, and the officers drive the men home in a car or truck. They are asked when it is convenient for them to appear in the office of the regional United States Magistrate (still called a Commissioner by moonshiners) for arraignment, and a time within the next few days is set. This type of arrangement between the moonshiner and the officers is most exceptional and does not appear in other forms of law enforcement. Experienced federal agents realize that the offender is a lawbreaker rather than a criminal, and fully understand this difference. After all, the purpose of law enforcement in this area is not the extermination of moonshiners but the ending of heavy losses in federal tax revenue. Almost without exception the moonshiner who agrees to appear does so on the dot with his bondsman, makes bond, and is released until trial. The older and more experienced revenue men actually know who can be trusted and who cannot, and while they do not hesitate to put a recalcitrant or unscrupulous moonshiner in jail immediately, it is unusual for them to do so. The moonshiner is proud that his integrity is known and that his word is good. Once he is arrested, tried, and convicted, he usually makes a model prisoner in a federal penitentiary.

In raiding the still all kinds of techniques are used. It is customary to investigate the site well in advance before planning a raid. Although small operations will be visited and destroyed, the agents' real interest is in the larger and steadily producing stills whose output costs the government heavily in lost tax revenue. Any information that comes to the officers or is discovered in the field is carefully evaluated, and raids are planned accordingly.

One of the simplest and most reliable ways to locate outdoor stills is to visit the spots where stills have been in the past. Every young revenue officer has had passed down to him from his older colleagues all the lore collected over the years relative to which hollows are natural sites. Revenuers can recognize these sites immediately by the remains of old masonry furnaces in which previous stills have been bedded.

Often the still is staked out in advance to be sure that whiskey is being produced, and the approach to the still is made slowly and quietly, each officer knowing exactly what he is to do. Sometimes the lookout spots the raiders or they betray themselves by noise or footprints, and the raid must be aborted because the moonshiners evaporate. The raid itself lasts only a few moments and sometimes only a few seconds. If it is well organized and conducted the officers appear as if by magic in the center of operations and begin grabbing the moonshiners. They may say, "This is the law," but usually the moonshiners are well aware of the fact; they submit, produce identity, and are booked on the spot. Occasionally they resist and a fist fight will ensue, but after the arrest is over relations between the moonshiners and the officers improve rapidly. In the old days shootings were common during still raids, and they are not entirely unknown today. There are usually firearms—often a shotgun or two used largely for signaling purposes—at the still site, and some harebrained youngster might be foolish enough to try to shoot it out.

On the whole, however, shootings are rare, and a kind of tacit understanding exists between agents and moonshiners that makes the work of each group easier, safer, and more humane.

After the raid the men are arraigned and usually represented by good lawyers. They are tried in federal court and before a federal judge who, in Kentucky, is likely to be quite familiar with the attitudes and philosophy of moonshiners and tempers the application of the law with this understanding. First offenders are often probated for six months or a year in the hope that weekly sessions with a probation officer will separate them from the moonshine business temporarily. When a first offender goes to federal prison he is eligible for parole after serving a third of his sentence, hence the "four months and sixteen days and they gonna turn me loose" of song and poem, the sixteen days being "processing time." If he is not eligible, he must serve nine months of the year or eighteen months out of two years before parole. Second- and third-time offenders may get a year and a day to two years, which they can serve out in five to seven or eight months. In prison they are usually assigned to the farm, where they are very much at home, and do not become custodial problems. Third- and fourth-time offenders may get as much as three to four years, but sentences of this length are not routine. In prison the moonshiner has certain advantages. He probably gets much better medical and dental care than he has had in his life. He eats a simple but wholesome diet, does not assault his liver with his own product, learns something about modern farming methods, and, best of all, meets other moonshiners who often know more about the craft than he does. So he attends open-ended informal seminars where the fine points of the whiskey traffic are explored and debated among men seasoned by years of solid experience. It is almost a foregone conclusion that when a still is raided and the papers of the men are examined, someone will have in

94

his wallet a laboriously traced pencil sketch of a new kind of still set-up that he has acquired from someone in federal prison.

As urban life has encroached upon the rural domain in Kentucky, there has been a natural tendency to put stills under cover and especially in buildings of various kinds. To the old-time moonshiner the thought of a still in a house would have been ridiculous, but since Prohibition the tendency to put stills in buildings has increased. While this of course obviates the kinds of camouflage necessary outdoors, it also demands certain techniques of concealment indigenous to a more gregarious kind of life. Sometimes moonshiners put stills in abandoned dwellings, or even in inhabited ones—where the traffic from trucks and cars does not attract attention, smoke rising from a chimney is natural, and supplies may be delivered and whiskey picked up without attracting too much attention. The problem of disposal of slops is easily solved by piping them underground or through a surface tile to the barn lot where they are used to feed pigs, cattle, and chickens. Naturally the presence of a still in a home is likely to throw domestic order and tranquility into disarray, but if a man insists on having a still in his home, he must live with it. Domestic stills also have the advantage of being workable at night. However, such stills have a relatively short industrial life since eventually the owner and his family are obliged to move to other quarters where the air is fresher and living is possible. Some farm families operate small coffin stills skillfully designed to fit over two burners of a gasoline or kerosene stove; these may produce a gallon or two a day over a period of many years without being detected. Small stills of this sort do not create the massive sanitation problems that accompany major moonshining operations in a house.

Outbuildings around farmhouses are often used with no sense of propriety regarding their original purpose. Even the lowly privy has been known to house a small

95

rig. Abandoned chicken coops, brooder houses, and corncribs can be used temporarily at least to house small stills. An old smokehouse is ideal since smoke issuing from it attracts no notice. Similarly, larger stills, especially steam stills, can be found in tobacco barns where during the winter months it is customary to use heat to cure the tobacco. Sometimes these are run only during the tobacco curing season, then dismantled and stored in the loft until the coming year.

In numerous small towns in Kentucky it is fashionable to keep the still in the cellar; this is usually not the case in the farmhouse, where drainage is a problem and the storage of crops and supplies is involved. Also, isolated farmhouses usually do not have cellars of any size. In the small towns, however, basements are of stone or poured concrete with water or sewage facilities built in. Therefore the installation of a still is tempting to someone with a knowledge of the craft and a market for moonshine. The pollution generated by a still under these conditions is less fearful than that in an isolated farmhouse, and with proper maintenance the existence of a still can be concealed for some time. The odor from fermentation and distillation, however, is a constant hazard, and stills in houses in town are almost invariably restricted to areas where the community offers a strong blanket of protection. One or two such typical communities lie in Nelson County, for instance. While very occasionally a moonshine still may be found in larger cities like Lexington, Frankfort, Ashland, or Louisville, this is indeed a rare occurrence, though bootlegging is not uncommon in these places.

Minimal external camouflage is not necessary for a still housed in a building, although precautions are taken to see that outsiders do not enter and that the activities of stilling cannot be observed from the outside. There is also the necessity of protection from the local police officers or sheriff, any or all of whom may have a slight financial interest in the production cycle. Federal

Jujus used to protect a
moonshine still; made of
gourds, corncobs, bits of
shell and plastic. From
central Kentucky.

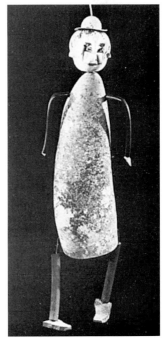

Fifty-gallon wooden barrel fermenters at a stream-side still site. *Bureau of Alcohol, Tobacco, and Firearms, U.S. Department of Treasury.*

Outdoor still seized near Pineville, Kentucky.

Bureau of Alcohol, Tobacco, and Firearms, U.S. Department of Treasury.

Quinn Pearl, an old-time federal revenue
agent, engaged in enforcement activities.
*Reprinted with permission from The Courier-Journal
and The Louisville Times.*

agents raid these stills when they know about them, but since they are located in communities where popular opinion favors the moonshiner and is hostile to the federal law, word travels very rapidly when the federal agents either investigate or arrive for a raid, so the results are not always successful.

It is notable that whenever Kentucky labor migrates into industrial cities of the North, moonshine stills appear in the most improbable neighborhoods, and local residents are suddenly blessed with a homemade product sufficiently explosive to make Saturday night a gala occasion. These stills are often financially successful, since in a neighborhood of unskilled laborers there is frequently a ready-made market for cheap, potent liquor.

The same officers who raid the stills usually carry out enforcement on the roads. In former years, these men had some chance to catch the whiskey transporters only if they were fortunate enough to confiscate souped-up cars from other conveyors. If not, they were due for long periods of frustration, since the government took a dim view of spending money to soup up cars. Today hot cars can be readily purchased commercially. However, since the transporter usually moves at very high speed when he is loaded and does not allow any car to stay long in his rearview mirror, it is difficult for agents to join in the chase even if they know a certain transporter is to appear on a certain highway at a particular time. By the time they have gotten the car onto the road and up to the speed of the transporter, he is long gone. Transporters often have a set of signals on a given highway or in some towns to warn them of the presence of officers, and of course until the officers discover and decode the signals they are at a continued disadvantage. Nevertheless, a considerable amount of illicit whiskey is confiscated each year by agents who dare to compete with the transporters at high speeds on unfamiliar roads. A considerable amount of this pursuit work is done at night, increasing the hazards for the agents. While the transporter has hazards as well, he has the advantage of knowing the terrain and can often drive at very high speeds with his lights turned off. The transporters are usually armed with a pistol, which they seldom attempt to use if captured, though there may be some shooting at tires by both parties while the chase is on. Sentences for transporters generally parallel those for moonshiners, though they may be tempered according to the quantity transported.

The field agents also have responsibility for locating and discouraging dealers in raw materials who supply moonshiners directly. Therefore they check shipping records of sugar wholesalers, food store operators, grain elevators, dealers in pipe and metal parts, and the like, in order to pinpoint large sales or shipments of these commodities to known moonshine areas. It is not usual policy to arrest the dealers who sell these materials without the existence of what the court calls strong probable cause. Ordinarily, however, it suffices to confer with and point out to a dealer the legal hazards to which he is exposing himself by selling large amounts of raw materials to known moonshiners. This may cause him to mend his ways, but more often he only finds a friend or relative who will handle the deal for him and protect his customer.

Since Prohibition days the federal enforcement staff has changed into a well-trained, well-disciplined, effective group of law enforcement officers highly motivated and thoroughly dedicated to their work. Regardless of any sentiment that Kentuckians may feel for the poor moonshiner, these agents contribute heavily not only to the protection of the federal tax revenues, but also to the health and sanity of Kentucky citizens. It is also significant that they protect the interests of the numerous and excellent legitimate distillers that contribute substantially to the economic welfare of Kentucky, for legitimate distillers find it difficult to compete with moonshiners who have an advantage of more than $10.00 in taxes on each gallon of whiskey they produce and sell.

In recent years there has been a dramatic decline in the number of stills seized in Kentucky. Several reasons account for this, the chief one being that the number of operating stills has been steadily reduced. In the early 1950s moonshining reached its peak of production in the state, probably surpassing the high levels of Prohibition times. By 1956 agents had seized over 25,000 stills nationwide, and in that year the federal government estimated that fifty million gallons more or less were produced and sold, involving a heavy loss in federal taxes. At that time, Kentucky ranked behind Tennessee, Alabama, the Carolinas, Georgia, and Florida in the number of stills seized. The total number of stills has declined sharply, until in 1968 there were only 336 seizures in Kentucky and in 1971, 82. This does not mean of course that only 82 stills were in operation, since by no means are all stills raided and destroyed. It may be estimated that one in five of those stills operating is seized. This estimate, however, will vary according to the location of the federal officers and the proximity to the time when federal budgets are approved by Congress.

Perhaps the number of stills seized or the gallons of untaxed liquor destroyed is not the only index to distilling activity. The number of people involved is also indicative, and it is interesting to note that during 1955–1957 more individuals were convicted on moonshine charges and sent to federal prison from Kentucky than from any other state. These figures break down as follows:

	Eastern district of Kentucky	Western district of Kentucky	Total
1955	266	121	387
1956	231	104	335
1957	254	100	354

These figures do not include the very large number of convictions that resulted in probation or a fine without imprisonment. Neither do they reflect the considerable number of violators who were arrested but against whom evidence was not sufficient for conviction. They do reflect, however, the vigorous and effective enforcement work done in Kentucky by federal officers at that time.

Federal agents estimate that in 1971 over twelve million gallons of untaxpaid whiskey were produced nationally by the stills captured; and Kentucky ranked only eighth or ninth in the number of stills seized. This is a far cry from 1954 when the federal government estimated that some 20 percent of all whiskey sold was illicit and untaxpaid. Perhaps this percentage becomes more significant when we·consider that Kentucky ranked very high in the production of licensed whiskey. Furthermore, it is the rare still that runs continuously. Ninety-five percent of them run only sporadically. It must be remembered that many of the stills raided are small and have slight production, while a relatively small number of the large ones with high production are seized. While fewer stills are seized today, among those that are seized is an increasing proportion of very large stills with a high individual output of illegal whiskey. Heavily producing stills are usually well financed, well concealed, and well protected so that they can operate more or less continuously.

Any statement on enforcement in Kentucky would be incomplete without the mention of state and local enforcement. On a state level, enforcement is under the direction of the Commissioner of Alcoholic Beverages; he maintains a small force of field agents who occasionally raid stills. More often these agents are interested in arresting local bootleggers. The main function of the commissioner is to enforce state laws governing the retail sale of alcoholic beverages through licensed dealers. These include hotels, bars, restaurants, cafés, beer depots, liquor stores, drug stores, and such. This department is also concerned with the observation of legal closing hours, the employment of certain types of personnel, and the rather widespread sale of either moonshine or legal liquor after hours on licensed or unlicensed premises.

The position of the state enforcement arm can be easily understood in terms of the following factors. First, the profits for dealers in bootlegging legal liquor are ever more attractive, thus diminishing moonshine traffic. Second, the state government is inclined to wink at such violations, the attitude being that if the tax is paid, forget it and permit the licensees to make some money in the business for which they are licensed. Third, in state court, conviction for moonshining is unlikely. Fourth, the Alcoholic Beverage Commission (ABC) is equipped in neither personnel, training, nor facilities to compete with the federal government. And fifth, many ex-moonshiners and moonshine bootleggers are turning toward illegal traffic in legal liquor, thus bypassing state interference.

Enforcement on the local level in Kentucky, while of some interest to both state and federal officers, is very heavily influenced by the sheriff of each county. In counties where the rural citizens are known to be "agin" liquor, production is usually low, and the local sheriff may take a more tolerant view and prefer not to know too much about production. It has been rumored that there are sheriffs or their deputies in certain Kentucky counties who have a small monetary interest in moonshine production. Sometimes this is indirect, through relatives or trusted friends who enjoy a kind of ephemeral monopoly during the tenure of certain officers. However, local sheriffs in Kentucky have a strong sense of responsibility to the people who elect them, and their enforcement policies tend in general to reflect the desires of their constituents.

In light of the severe decline in moonshine production, in the number of stills operating, and the number of people involved, it is obvious that the industry is at its lowest ebb since pre-Prohibition days. A number of factors are involved in this decline. First, the market has tapered off, since many younger people are now holding jobs in business and industry, able to purchase taxpaid whiskey, and ultimately learning to prefer it. Second, improved enforcement methods and more efficient enforcement personnel have over the past fifteen years had a heavy impact on the number of stills operating and the number of men willing to take the increased risk. Third, moonshining is today largely in the hands of older men who are becoming less and less active. In past years young boys and men learned moonshining by helping their fathers at the still. The craft passed from generation to generation, each proud of its reputation for quality. As the larger syndicates or combines have moved into the moonshining business, there has been little place for young boys. Consequently, there is small opportunity for young men to learn the craft and take their place in a new generation of distillers. Hence the production and consumption of moonshine tends to be less common in the more prosperous rural and small town areas, while incidences of both production and consumption are higher in the poorer classes and more isolated areas. While this generalization is not universally true, it has been observed as a pattern by various people who keep in touch with the situation. Furthermore, during the past fifteen years there has been a spectacular change in the highway system in Kentucky. Many formerly remote areas are now quite accessible to outsiders, and the relative isolation in which moonshine flourished is being broached.

Another significant factor in the decline of moonshine as an industry has been the decline of moonshine quality, due to the aforementioned development of syndicates and large-scale shipments of the product to areas outside the center of production. In fact, pride in quality has been diluted in direct proportion to the expansion of distribution.[1]

Winds of change are also blowing in the land. In former days it was considered quite a lark for lively young men to pool their cash, buy a few quart jars of moonshine whiskey, and consume it at a dance, play-party, athletic contest, or nighttime fox hunt. Today more sophisticated forms of entertainment are accessible in most parts of Kentucky. The drive-in movie, the basketball game, the high school dance, and gatherings at local drive-in restaurants are not always compatible with the purchase and consumption of moonshine whiskey. In addition, teenage girls play more and more of a part in the recreational pattern of young men, and this changes the tenor of the fun; the delights of contraband whiskey consumed in the company of other young bucks diminishes in attraction for mixed groups of young people. Because of cultural factors and the liquor's taste, few girls drink moonshine whiskey with pleasure. However, beer is usually available even in dry territory and this lighter drink may be shared by boys and girls, resulting in a general upgrading of interpersonal relations. Then, too, the general availability of soft drinks of many kinds makes the consumption of moonshine less common; in fact, when moonshine is consumed today, it is very often mixed with a cola drink and taken as a highball, a practice that must cause many old-time moonshiners to turn gently in their graves.

There is also a new factor involved in the decline of moonshine as a popular drink. This is the increasing use of drugs among younger people, and unfortunately most of the small towns in Kentucky have a burgeoning drug culture. Many of the younger people who twenty years ago would have been whooping it up on moonshine are now playing with marijuana, amphetamines, methadrine (speed), the barbiturates, or heroin.

The knowledge of the ancient craft of illegal distilling persists in the culture, however. It is deeply imbedded

103

through practice and tradition over a period of centuries. A decline in production, a reduction in the number of stills seized, and a tendency away from moonshine by a new generation do not mean that the craft will die. It will still be practiced at the heads of lonesome hollows flush with limestone spring water and plenty of firewood. The tradition will be kept alive in the hands of a diminishing few, but it will never disappear. The time may come when changing economic conditions, a shift in recreational patterns, the unavailability of legal liquor, and other shifts in life patterns will bring moonshine into favor again. Then the old copper pot stills will be sought out from barn lofts, kegs and barrels will be shaped to the need, copper coils will be replaced, and a new generation will experience the supreme joy of thumbing its nose at the Establishment.

8

THE ARGOT OF
THE CRAFT

*Zounds! I was never so
bethump'd with words . . .*
SHAKESPEARE, *King John*

ALL SUBCULTURES TEND to develop some specialized linguistic characteristics that set their members
apart from the general cultural matrix to which they
belong. When this subculture operates outside the law,
this linguistic phenomenon is called *argot*. Some of the
social and psychological forces that stimulate differen-
tial linguistic development can be very simply stated.
First, there is a dichotomy with the dominant culture,
with the subculture being quite aware—sometimes over
a period of centuries—of its minority status. Second, the
subculture differs from the dominant culture in some
(though never all) behavioral indices. For instance,
often there is within the subculture one or more occupa-
tions that are exclusive and somewhat secretive. There
are differences in ethics and moral values. The status of
women may vary from that in the dominant culture, as
well as concepts of time and territoriality. Patterns of association and interaction are sometimes different from
those of the dominant culture. There is a strong sense of
the "in-group."

When the subculture is a criminal one, there is hostility toward the dominant culture, hostility that is reciprocated and often expressed in terms of laws designed to control the subculture. In turn, this suppression causes the subculture to strengthen its internal security and to further differentiate itself from the dominant culture. Without some external pressure, criminal subcultures do not develop beyond the rudimentary or abortive stage. The threat from the dominant culture intensifies the internal forces already at work and tends to accentuate the values, attitudes, and techniques of the subgroup, at the same time fostering disparagement of those outside; the special aspects of their language reflect these forces. Improvements in criminal technology intensify this linguistic activity, often with the emphasis on secrecy. The gap between culture and subculture widens. As a criminal subculture becomes more aware of its functional identity, a self-image is generated that must be bolstered by word and deed, and the argot becomes a prime factor not only in the transmission of criminal techniques, but in triggering criminal behavior as well. This glorified self-image may be confused with reality, while the argot constantly serves to enhance prestige and to gratify ego-expansion.

Professional criminal subcultures are consistently parasitic, and agglutinate against the matrix of a legitimate society already vastly experienced in symbolizing its values through language. The subgroups tend to draw words and phrases from the contiguous language, rather than creating many neologisms, and to give these established words new and special meanings. This makes for group solidarity, mutual recognition, and a sense of exclusiveness. It is significant that criminal subcultures seem to evolve against such a body of specialized language, and that both the subculture and the argot proliferate in response to the interplay of the forces mentioned above. I have examined this phenomenon in detail in various other studies bearing on specific subcultures of professional criminals.

While the moonshiners commit their crimes against the law rather than against persons or property, they nevertheless constitute a criminal subculture with many of the characteristics thereof. This subculture was made criminal by law, however, and not by any vicious or vindictive behavior. It is interesting in that its criminal activity is largely confined to violation of the liquor laws; in most other respects it blends with a conservative agricultural society. This compatibility between the law violators and legitimate agricultural life has prevailed in both England and America for nearly 300 years. Almost always, moreover, this society, on a local level, in general approves of moonshining and tends to protect the violators who live there as long as they cooperate with those in political power.

In addition to the factors already mentioned, the subculture of the moonshiner in Appalachia had a long history of breaking European laws considered unjust. Scotsmen and Irishmen had no scruples about evading taxes levied by the British Crown long before it began to tax illicit whiskey. They were specialists in poaching and smuggling, and the strong "Geneva waters" (later called gin) from the Continent was just one of the products they imported duty-free. In fact, the word moonshine referred to any smuggled goods, and then to smuggled liquor, well before it was particularized to strong drink made illegally at home. The Scotch and Irish found many an English farmer in Northumberland, as well as English seamen out of Glasgow and Belfast, who liked to play the smuggler's game. The stock that migrated to Appalachia already had generations of experience at expert law violation, heavily concentrated in the area of the making and transporting of liquor. In fact, they made and drank it long before it was taxed.

This stock brought to America something that most criminal subcultures do not have—a genuine and ancient mystique. In Scotland and Ireland the process of fermentation of grain had been a part of sacred Gaelic fertility rites since long before the Romans occupied Britain. A thousand years later, after the alchemists introduced the still from Arabia, the making of alcohol was surrounded with an aura of magic and mystery that characterized the highly secret activities of alchemy. In colonial America and the Caribbean, where slaves were used in some areas as still labor, perhaps touches of African magic were incorporated. Primitive animistic beliefs, which we would refer to today as superstitions, still permeate the subculture, and remnants of them linger as the carefully guarded trade secrets of portions of the modern legitimate distilling industry.

This heritage probably intensified the social and psychological factors that account for the development of a semisecret argot. Today the speech patterns of the moonshine subculture are indistinguishable from those of the immediate geographical area to which it is indigenous; phonologically and syntactically there is nothing to set a moonshiner off from others in the broad agricultural community. These patterns have been recorded very precisely by many linguistic researchers, notably those of the *Linguistic Atlas of the United States and Canada*. However, the moonshiner has had something else: a lexicon associated with his craft known to all members of the subculture almost exclusively. It is notable that, among the literally thousands of dialect terms collected by linguistic geographers, very few words and phrases from this argot appear. In very recent years, however, linguistic diffusion seems to have begun, old taboos seem to have weakened, and within the past two years some terms from the moonshine subculture have begun to appear in various forms of "country" music that exploit the Appalachian culture in general. Previously a small amount of the argot had appeared in fiction.

The content of this lexicon is rather a mixed bag. One might expect that the technical language used by Appalachian moonshiners would go back to Scotch-Irish sources dating from the eighteenth century. It is probable that some of it does, and that these elements were dialectal or nonstandard at the time. It is also possible that some of the vocabulary used by moonshiners in the United States dates back beyond the eighteenth century. In other words, the craft may have evolved along two lines, overlapping to some extent, but with one line following ancient folk traditions—ultimately illicit—and the other developing with the standard industrial distilling activities—largely legal—that arose in Great Britain during this period. Undoubtedly early Continental technological influences were strong in this development. This situation might well be paralleled today in Kentucky, where moonshining persists as a craft in the hands of people using older folk methods, while the modern legal industry has grown up in the same area, inheriting some of the ancient folklore, but increasingly dominated by scientific technology.

All this is speculation, based on a rather superficial examination of notes taken in the field. The entire language of distilling, both licit and illicit, in both the United States and Great Britain, deserves to be studied in depth. Such a study might well untangle these threads and give us a documented picture of the diachronic elements involved. The connections to Scotch-Irish and even Gaelic dialects are obscure; at the same time the relationship of the moonshiner's language to that of standard legal distilling is looser and less specific than we might expect.

During the eighteenth century legal distilling in Europe reached a rather sophisticated level. I have consulted some of the rather specialized works dealing with this period, notably the exhaustive *Practical Treatise on Brewing, Distilling, and Rectification* by R. Shannon, M.D. (London, 1805). This voluminous work describes traditional practices standardized during the previous century, includes precise diagrams of equipment, and cites as well the technical language used in England, Scotland, Ireland, the West Indies, and on the Continent. There has been relatively little transference of this language to the idiom of modern Kentucky moonshiners. In fact, modern moonshiners seem to share only some basic rudiments of terminology for methods and equipment, such as *worm, coil, malt, mash, mash tub, vat, double, double back, backings, beer, beer cap.* Apparently lost to American moonshiners is the bulk of the older vernacular, some of it smelling of the colorful terminology of alchemy.

Two other influences on the moonshiners' usage should be mentioned. The first of these is the terminology used in modern legal distilling, especially in the smaller distilleries where tradition lingers heavily. Even this influence is not so strong as we might expect, in view of the commercial distilleries' proximity to moonshine areas and the fact that many moonshiners have at one time been employed as still labor. Some terms are of course borrowed, but more typical perhaps is what happened in the case of such a device as the dephlegmator. The moonshiners observed the dephlegmator working, made a crude replica of their own, rejected the technical term as too fancy, and produced their own name for it, which was *puker*, with a derivative transitive verb *to puke*, as in "You get the fire a mite too hot and you puke the still." The American moonshiner seems to have most frequently adapted nontechnical dialect words already familiar and created neosemanticisms in preference to adopting a more technical vocabulary in connection with his craft.

The second influence is what we might loosely call "the underworld" of Prohibition days; during this time, many moonshiners came into contact with urban gangsters. Since most of these contacts were with rum-runners, a few terms from this subculture were adopted, largely in the transportation end of the industry.

Following is a glossary of terms found among Kentucky moonshiners. While it is not complete, it has been carefully prepared and gives an overview of the terms presently used in the manufacture, sale, and distribution of illicit whiskey in large quantities. It should be noted that there is also a somewhat smaller and partially overlapping vocabulary used by bootleggers, of whom there appears to be at least one in every sizable Kentucky community; these terms have been largely omitted except where they overlap the usage of moonshiners proper.

Glossary

alky *n*. (1) Illegal beverage alcohol. Not in general use among moonshiners, but used by bootleggers and wholesalers who distribute illegal liquor. (2) A grade of moonshine which, although of poor quality, is high-proof stuff to be cut by an equal amount of water. Used especially by those operators with experience during Prohibition.

alky column *n*. A crude but effective column still for making illicit whiskey on a large scale. Mostly found in large, urban areas where syndicates control illicit liquor. Unknown to rural moonshiners.

backer *n*. A third person or associated party who owns and/or finances moonshine operations.

backings or **backins** *n*. Low-proof liquor, not containing enough alcohol to be considered whiskey. Usually low-proof distillate near the end of a run. ". . . about a gallon backins left in the thumper." Compare SINGLINGS.

bead *n*. The little bubbles that form along the meniscus of liquor when shaken in a bottle, allowing an experienced moonshiner to judge the proof and quality of the liquor with great accuracy. "This stuff holds a good bead." *intr. v.* To form bubbles and hold them around the surface periphery, as liquor tends to do. "This don't bead so good."

beading oil *n*. Oil added to low-proof liquor to make the bead appear as if the liquor were 100 proof. This practice, a survival from Prohibition days, is frowned upon by both moonshiners and bootleggers. "When the bootleggers get it, they'll slip a little beading oil in it and two parts water."

113

beer *n.* Fermented mash, either grain or sugar. "That beer's working off good." Also called "still-beer."

beer still *n.* The still in which the beer is cooked to separate the spirits (low-proof alcohol) from the residue. In some areas this same still is then used to redistill the spirits to make whiskey. "We just got one more charge of beer. You put it in the beer still while I. . . ."

big fellow *n.* A federal law-enforcement officer. In Central Kentucky, moonshiners make little distinction between branches of the law, largely because all enforcement officers wear rough clothes instead of uniforms when making raids. "We best pull out. The big fellows was by here today." Also called "Feds," "The Law," "Marshal," "Prohi," "Revenoo."

blubber *n.* The froth created when moonshine and beading oil are shaken in a temping bottle.

boiler *n.* An enclosed vessel in which water is boiled to generate steam for a steam still. It may be anything from an old oil drum, with crude fittings, to a standard upright, factory-made steam boiler with gauges, fittings, safety devices, etc. ". . . boiler blowed up and kilt three of 'em."

box *n.* See FERMENTER.

break *intr. v.* Used of the distillate. To drop to a low proof, indicating that the beer is becoming exhausted in the still. The moonshiner often says that the liquor "breaks at the worm" or "breaks at the coil" since he becomes aware of the drop of proof at this point.

break up *tr. v.* To sift the scalded mass of meal through a coarse screen (usually hardware cloth) in order to remove the lumps. Part of the mashing operation. "Tomorrow we'll break up them barrels and set in." "We got to break up that scalded meal."

bulldog *tr. v.* To heat used barrels by setting them against a large oil drum in which a fire is built in order to sweat out the whiskey that has soaked into the barrel staves. In some areas a slower process involves setting closed barrels in hot sunlight. ". . . bulldog them barrels and get ten gallons of likker." Also "to dog," "to sweat."

burner *n.* A kerosene or gasoline heating unit for cooking mash or distilling liquor. Usually used with steam stills. "That old burner roars till I can't hear what you're saying."

can *n.* (1) In the Southern mountains, a half-gallon fruit jar. Also called "glass can." (2) In other districts, a five- to ten-gallon wood-covered metal container. Also called "jacket," or "jacket can." (3) A G.I. or jerry can (a postwar addition); one of the Army's five-gallon gasoline cans adapted to distilling needs. While the "glass can" and "jacket can" are usually used only to hold liquor, the G.I. cans may be set aside for kerosene or gasoline. However, large shipments of liquor are often made exclusively in G.I. cans, "Only time I was ever caught. . . . Had ten jacket cans." "Set that can of likker over here."

cap *n.* (1) The cover, usually of copper, that is placed over the opening in the top of the still through which vapor passes via the connections to the condenser. "You put the cap on and I'll put the paste to her." (2) The frothy formation on the top of the vat of fermenting beer that finally clears away, settling through the beer. "It ain't ready to run. The cap ain't broke."

catch-can *n.* The receptacle that receives the distillate from the terminal of the flakestand. Usually a five-gallon can or bucket.

charge *n.* One filling of the still from the fermenter vats. "We only lacked one charge of being through." "We can run a charge an hour." *tr. v.* To fill the still with beer.

chips *n.* Oak chips added to liquor to give it color and congeners in one method of quick aging. Usually done in kegs or barrels. "We can throw a handful of chips in that and get more for it." See also QUICK AGING. Compare NEEDLING.

clear *intr. v.* Used of the cap of meal on top of the fermenter. To break and settle to the bottom, leaving the beer relatively clear. "Quick as that beer clears, we'll run it."

coffin still *n.* A small still designed to fit over two burners of a gasoline or kerosene stove.

coil *n.* A type of condenser, usually made of twenty to forty feet of copper tubing coiled within a barrel of cold water. "That coil's sixty foot long." Also called "worm." See also CONDENSER. Compare STRAIGHT-CONDENSER.

collar *n.* The copper band or ring connecting the cap and the still.

condenser *n.* Copper tubing used to condense alcohol vapor. Sometimes one tube enclosed within another of larger diameter. "That condenser acts like they ain't no baffles in it." See also COIL, STRAIGHT-CONDENSER.

connections *n.* The copper parts that join the still or still-cap to the thump-keg, and the thump-keg to the condenser. "The connections are what's hard to make."

cooker *n.* (1) The beer still proper. (2) A tank or box used to precook beer.

copper *n.* (1) STILL POT (*see*). (2) CONDENSER (*see*). (3) Any copper part of the moonshiner's equipment. "Pull out the copper and leave the rest be."

corn liquor *n.* (1) Among moonshiners, used to mean liquor made with some corn, usually from one peck to one bushel per barrel of mash, the balance of which is sugar or, more rarely, some other grain. (2) In selling, used to mean liquor made from pure (100 percent) corn, which is rare indeed. Also called "straight corn." (3) Any untaxed moonshine liquor. Intonation often reflects the degree to which corn is actually used. "You got any corn likker?" "This ain't sugar likker, this is corn likker." "Shore, that's corn likker." Compare SUGAR LIQUOR.

crash car *n.* (1) A junker that can be abandoned in an emergency. (2) Widely used in Prohibition days, now rare in Kentucky, an escort car that follows or precedes a liquor transporter for purposes of protection.

dock *n.* A term used in Lyon and Trigg counties, Kentucky, for the still equipment. "They's two docks over on Stinkin' Crick."

dog *tr. v.* to BULLDOG (*see*).

dog head *n.* A large viscous bubble that forms in the still just before the cap is sealed.

doggins *n.* Liquor obtained from used barrels by the process of bulldogging.

double or **double back** *v.* To remash at the same place, in the same vats, using the slops from the preceding distillation as a part of the mash. "We doubled back and made a good run." Also "to mash back."

doubler *n.* A processing keg, placed between the still and the flakestand, that redistills the liquor by using the heat of the vapor itself, thus eliminating the need to distill twice or use separate stills. "Listen to that old doubler chuckle." Also called "thumper," "thump-keg."

doublings *n.* (*plural only*). The complete cycle that is made by running fermented beer through a still, extracting the alcohol, and doubling or mashing back. "Yeah, we made ten doublings at that place."

faints *n.* (1) Low-proof distillate that comes through the condenser at the end of a run. Also called "tailings." Sometimes applied to weak FIRST SHOTS. (2) Heated slops used for setting mash.

Feds *n.* Officers of the Alcohol Tax Unit. "Yeah, the Feds got Bill and Luke." Also called "Revenoo," "Marshal," "Prohi," "The Law." See also BIG FELLOW.

117

fermenter *n.* A container in which the mash is set to ferment: a. *Tub,* often made of half barrels or square wooden vats. b. *Box,* a rectangular vat made from heavy boards bolted or nailed together. "That was a real set—six big boxes bubbling with beer."

field a bond *v. phr.* To make, fill, or get bond when arrested. Origin of this idiom is obscure. "Bill could help us field a bond." "If I can't field a bond, I'll rot in this damned place."

filter *n.* A strainer, usually of felt, though sometimes of other material, used to remove foreign matter or cloudiness from liquor. "Get that filter off the bush. This stuff's cloudy." *tr. v.* To strain the distillate. "You filter what's in the catch-can."

fire in the hole! *interj.* Local warning cry, especially on Coe Ridge in Cumberland County, Kentucky, and elsewhere near the Tennessee line, heard immediately after word has spread that the "law's in." Called in a high-pitched, far-carrying yodel, it is necessary to know the words in order to understand them. Adapted from the coal mines, where it is used to indicate that the fuse has been lit and a powder charge is about to explode. (In parts of Tennessee, especially in Cooke County, dynamite charges are set off as alarms; the explosions rocket through the valleys, reverberating for many seconds.)

first shots *n.* The initial distillate which emerges from the flakestand as the stilling process begins. This liquor is high in esters, aldehydes, and fusel oil that make it undrinkable. "This 'ere still yet runnin' first shots." Also called "heads," "foreshots."

flake or **flakestand** *n.* The container, filled with cold water, in which the condenser is immersed so that the alcohol vapor will condense. Usually a barrel or a drum.

foreshots *n.* FIRST SHOTS (*see*).

furnace *n.* A base made of field stone, clay, or mortar that houses the fire under a pot still, or under the boiler of a steam still.

get probate *v. phr.* To be placed on probation. Because there is no jail sentence involved, the defendant is considered by the community to have "beaten the case." Conviction on a moonshine charge carries no stigma, incidentally, in moonshining areas, most of which are "dry" by local option. "Naw, they never convicted Lem. He got probate."

glass can *n.* See CAN.

goose eye *n.* A perfect bead, indicating 100 proof.

go round *intr. v.* To distill and remash all of one's fermenters in sequence. Big-time operators consider it wise to run only a short time at one location and then move the still. The length of time is expressed not in days, but in *go rounds*. ". . . hell, we went round six times at that old spring." "Maybe we kin go round once more before we run out." *n.* DOUBLINGS (*see*).

guard *n.* The individual who gives warning in case of a raid. In some areas, distinction is made between the lookout, who gives the warning, and the guard whose job is to put up a fight. Carefully spaced shotgun blasts are universally employed throughout Kentucky as a warning.

heads *n.* FIRST SHOTS (*see*).

heater or **heater-box** *n.* Found only on large stills, a box into which beer is poured or pumped to be preheated. It uses heat from the liquor vapor to serve double duty as both dephlegmator and precooker. Heater-boxes occur in a wide variety of sizes, shapes, locations, and connections with a still, "Pump some beer in the heater-box, Joe." Also called "preheater."

high shots *n.* Very high-proof liquor which must be cut with water or backings to 100 proof.

horny-man *n.* Federal agent, a euphemism for devil.

horse-blanket whiskey *n.* A crude form of liquor made by covering a boiling kettle of beer with a heavy, folded horse-blanket. When the blanket is heavy with condensed moisture,

119

two men twist it to extrude the liquor. The process is then repeated. This technique is not approved by first-class moonshiners.

jacket or **jacket can** *n.* See CAN.

kerosene liquor *n.* Liquor contaminated by kerosene. A teaspoon of kerosene in a one thousand-gallon vat of beer will cause all the liquor to taste of kerosene. When kerosene is used to fire the boiler in a large steam still operation, the moonshiner must be extremely careful to wash his hands after filling the pressure tank, and not allow any of his supply bags to lean against a kerosene drum when hauling them to the still site. "Kerosene likker . . . sold me a pint of kerosene likker."

kick or **kicker** *n.* Any form of nitrate added to mash with the intent of increasing the yield.

law, the *n.* FEDS (*see*).

lime *tr. v.* To whitewash the inside of the fermenters to reduce contamination. "We got to lime them boxes."

lookout *n.* See GUARD.

low wines *n.* The low-proof liquor produced by the first distillation; the first run of the still.

malt corn, corn malt, or **sprouting malt corn** *n.* Universally used in the eastern Kentucky mountains, made by burying a sack of corn under damp leaves until the corn has sprouted, then grinding the sprouted grain. Used principally by small operators. Large operators buy barley malt in larger quantities. "Yeah, I got a gunny sack of malt corn sprouted."

marshal *n.* FEDS (*see*).

mash *n.* The mixture in the vats prior to or during fermentation. *tr. v.* To prepare ingredients for fermentation.

mashing in *intr. v.* (1) To put the ingredients in the vats for fermentation. (2) To begin the process of whiskey making. "We've got to finish mashing in before noon." See also MASH.

mash back *intr. v.* To DOUBLE BACK (*see*).

mash-floor *n.* A platform built adjacent to the vats (usually over a creek) on which the operator stands to stir the mash. "You ain't got a thing on me. I never set my foot on the mash-floor."

mash-stick *n.* A hardwood stick 1½ or 2 inches in diameter and from 5 to 8 feet long, pierced through at the lower end by several small sticks of different lengths. Used to stir mash to assure maximum conversion.

middlings *n.* A kind of livestock feed often used by moonshiners as a substitute for grain. ". . . used middlings because we didn't have no meal."

mud, mud in, or **mud up** *tr. v.* To build up the still furnace and smokestack with masonry. "You mud up the stack." "You mud it for me."

needling *gerund* A method of quick aging, used by some moonshiners, whereby an electric needle is inserted in the keg. The beneficial effects are questionable. "That ain't aged likker, it's needled."

outfit *n.* STILL (*see*).

paste *n.* A thick mixture of flour, rye, or meal, and water, used for sealing joints in the still connections to prevent the escape of vapor.

pot *n.* (1) A pot still with all of its accessories. (2) Variant of STILL-POT.

pot still *n.* See STILL.

pour up *tr. v.* To distribute moonshine (after it has been temped to 100 proof) into containers for distribution.

preheater *n.* HEATER (*see*).

pressure tank *n.* The container that supplies kerosene under pressure either to the burner under the still, or to a steam boiler. It is usually pumped with an ordinary tire pump or with an air compressor. "Pump up that pressure tank before the burner quits."

prohi [pronounced prohai] *n.* FEDS (*see*). *adj.* Federal or law enforcement. "Them goddam, low-down, sonuvabitch prohi bastards. . . ."

proof *n.* A term borrowed from legitimate distilling to indicate the percentage of alcohol in any distillate. One hundred proof distillate is 50 percent alcohol.

puke *tr. v.* To allow the still to boil over into the connections. This often necessitates dismantling the still and cleaning out the connections, the thump-keg, and the condenser. "Don't throw no more wood on that fire, you'll puke the still."

puker *n.* A primitive dephlegmator between the still and the thump-keg that returns any boiled-over mash to the still, thereby preventing it from contaminating the distillate.

pull out *intr. v.* (1) To take the still out of the furnace or stack, and hide or remove it. This is often done when operators suspect that the still has been reported. Also "to pull the still." (2) to quit stilling at that particular spot. (3) To remove all the most expensive equipment, especially the copper, and leave the location. "We got to pull out before he reports on us."

pull the fire *v. phr.* To remove the fire under the still (in pot-type operations) in order to stop the beer from boiling. The pot can then be emptied and refilled without danger from scalding steam. In copper pot operations, the fire must be pulled every time the charge is changed. The fire must also be pulled at the end of each operation or day of operation and carefully put out or scattered on the naked ground as a precaution against forest fires. "That's what takes the time, pullin' the fire every time you change a charge."

pull the still *v. phr.* To PULL OUT (*see*).

quick aging *gerund* Any method of giving color to liquor quickly and, of course, artificially. "That likker ain't old. It's just been quick aged." See also CHIPS, NEEDLING.

quill *n.* A straw used to sample beer in the vats. Still-beer is considered at its best for drinking just before distillation; however, it is drunk at almost every stage after it has begun to ferment. Passersby often slip in to sample it, although this practice is discouraged. "Hand me that quill. I'm fixing to drink some beer out of this barrel."

race *n.* The chase to escape law enforcement officers. It may be either by car or on foot. Such a chase is quite common, since federal officers seldom shoot first at violators of the liquor law. "Me and the law had a race." "I shore give the law a race yesterday."

raise yeast *v. phr.* To grow one's own yeast rather than buy it. There are interesting legends regarding the proper method of catching the "wild yeast" to get a start. In eastern Kentucky many moonshiners think they do not use yeast. They keep their fermentation going by using some old mash in each new batch, but do not know why. "We never bought no yeast. We raised our own yeast."

relay arm *n.* The connection between the relay barrel and the still through which heated beer is piped.

relay barrel or **keg** *n.* A large scale puker combined with a preheater arrangement for preheating beer and charging the still. Seldom used in Kentucky.

report or **report on** *v.* To inform the law of a liquor violation. "He reported on me." Also "to turn in," "to turn up."

revenoo, reveneuer or **revenooer** *n.* FEDS (*see*).

rig *n.* STILL (*see*).

run *v.* (1) To distill a batch of fermented beer. (2) To transport whiskey. *n.* A cycle of whiskey.

run out or **run (it) out** *v.* To finish distillation of the beer on hand and cease operation, either temporarily or permanently. "We're gonna run out and quit." "This set's hot, but we may have time to run it out." "When we run out, we'll move up the creek."

scald *tr. v.* In corn or part-corn operations, to cook the meal in preparation for making mash.

scorched liquor *n.* Liquor made from mash that has been allowed to burn at the bottom of the fermenter, or meal that has burned in the still-pot while being scalded. "This tastes like it's scorched likker."

screen *n.* A frame covered with coarse, wire netting through which scalded mash is sometimes worked to remove lumps.

set *n.* STILL (*see*). *tr. v.* (1) To scald mash and prepare it for fermentation. (2) To prepare the equipment and place the mash in the vats for fermentation. (3) To establish a still. Used intransitively in phrases like "to set up" and "to set in." "We got set in one Sunday and run a month."

settle *v.* To CLEAR (*see*). "The cap ain't broke up, let 'er settle."

shack *n.* (1) A makeshift shed in which the still is sometimes set. ". . . built a shack over the shine." (2) The storage shed for materials and supplies at a still.

shine *n.* A moonshine still.

sign *n.* (1) Tracks. (2) Evidence of moonshine traffic.

singlings *n.* Low-proof liquor that does not contain enough alcohol to be considered whiskey. This liquor has been run through the still only once in cases where two stills or two distilling operations are used. Also applied to the condensate in the thump-keg. "That ain't likker, that's jest singlin's." Compare BACKINGS.

slop or **slops** n. Exhausted still-beer.

slop mash n. Mash to which the stillage from the previous distillation has been added in order to get the benefit of whatever alcohol is left in the slop. This procedure usually follows the first mashing. "We ought to get a better turn-out from slop mash." See also MASH.

sour mash n. Mash made by scalding meal with hot slops, in contrast to *sweet mash* which is made by scalding the meal with fresh water.

spent beer or **spent mash** n. Beer, hot from the still, from which the alcohol has been exhausted. This is either discarded or used to set a new tier of fermenters.

splo n. Cheap low grade whiskey.

stack n. The rocks or bricks built around the still in pot operations, and the boiler in steam operations. "This still ain't been outa the stack for a month." *tr. v.* To set the still or the boiler up in masonry so that a fire can be applied. "You stack the still while I get the. . . ." See also MUD.

stash n. A cache of raw materials or liquor, usually not at the still site. "We got ninety gallon left in the stash."

steam still n. See STILL.

still n. The pot or container in which the beer is distilled to make whiskey. a. In *pot* operations, a small copper container. "We got us a fifty-gallon copper pot." b. In *steam* operations, a large vat, usually made of silo staves, but sometimes of metal. "That's a steamer. The still will hold five hundred gallons of beer."

still-beer n. Variant of BEER (*see*).

still-pot *n.* The metal body of the still in which the beer is cooked. ". . . old still-pot's about burnt up."

straight-condenser *n.* A straight piece of copper tubing laid in a trough of cold running water and used to condense alcohol vapor. Not common. Compare COIL.

straight corn *n.* See CORN LIQUOR.

sugar jack *n.* One hundred proof whiskey made from sugar without the addition of corn, except for a small amount to start and maintain fermentation.

sugar liquor *n.* Liquor made from sugar. "This ain't no good. It's sugar likker." Compare CORN LIQUOR.

sugar mash *n.* A sugar solution, sometimes mixed with a small amount of cornmeal, set to ferment into beer.

swab *n.* A long, hickory sapling, well frayed at one end and used along with the mash-stick to keep mash from sticking and scorching in the still. Sometimes to better get at the mash, a rag is tied to the end of the stick.

sweat *tr. v.* To BULLDOG (*see*).

sweet mash *n.* See SOUR MASH.

tailings *n.* FAINTS (*see*).

take the word *v. phr.* To spread the alarm of a pending raid. The signal may consist of two spaced gunshots. Often moonshiners send a runner with the message; "the word" of a stranger's approach travels with incredible rapidity. "Yeah, he took the word, else they'd got ketched Friday." "We got the word just in time to git gone."

temp *tr. v.* To test the bead on liquor by shaking it in a bottle in order to ascertain whether or not the liquor must be "tempered" by the addition of water or backings. If the liquor does not hold a bead, higher proof distillate must be added.

126

temping bottle *n.* A bottle in which a sample of liquor is placed and shaken to test the formation of the bead indicating the proof of the liquor. "Here, take that temping bottle and see how this stuff beads."

thumper or **thump-keg** *n.* DOUBLER (*see*). The term derives from the putt-putt thumping noise caused by steam in the keg.

trouble *n.* An arrest for liquor law violation. "Yeah, he's been in trouble before."

tub *n.* See FERMENTER.

turn-out *n.* Yield of whiskey per amount of corn or sugar used. "What turn-out did you get—ten gallons to the bag?" "We ain't gettin' no turn-out."

vat *n.* FERMENTER (*see*).

vat plug *n.* The plug in the drain hole of a fermenter. "Pull that vat plug and wash that box out."

water mash *n.* The first mash made in a stilling operation; since there is no spent stillage available, it is mixed with water. "We never got much turn-out on the water mash." See also MASH.

weed-monkey or **weed-mule** *n.* The old car or truck used to haul supplies to the still site and to transport liquor. Mostly Tennessee usage. "Take that old weed-monkey and go get the meal."

whiskey still *n.* A small auxiliary still (in addition to the beer still) used sometimes for rectifying low wines. "This little pot is big enough for a whiskey still."

worm *n.* COIL (*see*).

wort *n.* A mixture of malt, water, and sugar used as an infusion in still-beer to promote fermentation.

Notes

Chapter 2

1. *A New English Dictionary on Historical Principles* (Oxford: Clarendon, 1888).

2. John S. Farmer and William E. Henley, *Slang and Its Analogues* (New Hyde Park, N.Y.: University Books, 1966).

3. Harriette Arnow, *Flowering of the Cumberland* (New York: Macmillan and Co., 1963), p. 271.

4. Henry G. Crowgey, *Kentucky Bourbon: The Early Years of Whiskeymaking* (Lexington: University Press of Ky., 1971), pp. 134–40.

5. The evolution of legal bourbon is a complicated story, discussed at some length in Crowgey, *Kentucky Bourbon*, pp. 124–34.

6. Ibid., p. 100.

7. *United States Statutes at Large*, 3 (Boston: Little, Brown & Co., 1861): 152–58.

8. *United States Statutes at Large*, 12 (Boston: Little, Brown & Co., 1865): 446–53, 571. The sequence of taxation and the foundation of the Internal Revenue Service in 1862 is chronicled by Carr, *The Second Oldest Profession: An Informal History of Moonshining in America*, chap. 3.

9. There is a well-known formula among legitimate distillers for determining the yield per bushel of grain. First, the percentage of alcohol by volume in the beer is multiplied by two. Second, the number of gallons of beer is divided by the number of bushels of grain in the mash recipe. Result #1 is multiplied by Result #2, and the answer multiplied by 0.01. This gives the number of proof gallons per bushel. Oldtime moonshiners who made straight corn whiskey were not concerned with these precise figures. (When sugar is added to the beer, of course, the yield in terms of proof gallons per bushel is no longer valid.)

Chapter 3

1. Different moonshiners, of course, claim different yields, and a little bragging is never inappropriate. However, Jess Carr in his book, *The Second Oldest Profession*, p. 77, reports that in Virginia, corn seems to grow to an incredible strength. In a demonstration run, he records that from ten bushels of corn and "with good luck and a still that 'holds her cap,' one hundred and twenty gallons of grain whiskey will be the result." This appears to be a gargantuan operation in which one bushel of corn is set to ferment in each of ten one hundred and twenty-gallon fermenters. The moonshiner would distill this beer for two days and two nights, which commendable devotion and exertion might account for the astoundingly high yield of twelve gallons per bushel.

In all fairness, it may be that an editorial error (a substitution of "grain whiskey" for "low wines") might offer a partial explanation. But even so, the still operator merits a Nobel Prize in chemistry and the highest award ever given by the Distilled Spirits Institute of America. These awards may come posthumously, however, for Carr reports that the moonshiner is an invalid of eighty-seven years, "but his mind is very sharp." I should add that any moonshiner who can get more than three gallons of 100 proof whiskey from a bushel of corn is eligible for a merit badge.

2. Some commercial distillers using highly efficient equipment estimate that under a vacuum 100 percent alcohol boils at 78.3 degrees C., 95.5 percent alcohol by weight boils at 78.1 degrees C., and aqueous solutions containing less than 95.5 percent alcohol by weight boil at temperatures from 78.1 to 100 degrees C. Obviously, an application of such a precise formula to the manufacture of moonshine whiskey is unrealistic.

Chapter 4

1. In the southeastern region of the United States in 1971, 76,224 gallons of illegally distilled spirits were destroyed by federal, state, and local agents, while 2,650 gallons were destroyed in other states. U.S. Dept. of the Treasury, Internal Revenue Service, *Summary Statistics* (Washington, D.C., 1972).

Chapter 7

1. While physical disaster spread nationwide during Prohibition, the holocaust was occasionally centered in one area as a result of the bad practices of a sole moonshiner. Kellner, *Moonshine: Its History and Folklore,* p. 223, reports that one individual spread the following havoc: forty-one dead, four rendered sightless, and three hundred and fifty made seriously ill.

Bibliography

Alcohol and Tobacco: Summary Statistics. Internal Revenue Service, Treasury Department. Washington: 1972.

Arnow, Harriette S. *Flowering of the Cumberland.* New York: Macmillan and Company, 1963.

Arnow, Harriette S. *Seedtime on the Cumberland.* New York: Macmillan and Company, 1960.

Bodley, Temple. *History of Kentucky.* 4 volumes. Chicago: S. J. Clarke Publishing Company, 1928.

Butler, Mann. *A History of the Commonwealth of Kentucky.* Berea: Oscar Rucker, Jr., 1969.

Carr, Jess. *The Second Oldest Profession: An Informal History of Moonshining in America.* Englewood Cliffs, New Jersey: Prentice-Hall, Inc., 1972.

Clark, Thomas D. *A History of Kentucky.* New York: Prentice-Hall, Inc., 1937. (Revised edition, Lexington: The John Bradford Press, 1950.)

Clark, Thomas D. *Kentucky: Land of Contrast.* New York: Harper and Row, 1968.

Collins, Lewis. *Historical Sketches of Kentucky.* Maysville: Lewis Collins and J. A. & U. P. James, Cincinnati, 1847. (Revised edition, Collins, Lewis and Collins, Richard H. *Collins' Historical Sketches of Kentucky.* 2 volumes. Covington: Collins & Company, 1874.)

Connelley, William E. and Coulter, E. M. *History of Kentucky.* 5 volumes. Chicago: The American Historical Society, 1922.

Crowgey, Henry G. *Kentucky Bourbon: The Early Years of Whiskeymaking.* Lexington: The University Press of Kentucky, 1971.

Davenport, F. Garvin. *Antebellum Kentucky: A Social History 1800–1860.* Oxford, Ohio: The Mississippi Valley Press, 1943.

Farmer, John S. and Henley, William E. *Slang and Its Analogues.* New Hyde Park, N.Y.: University Books, 1966.

The Foxfire Book. Edited by Eliot Wiggington. Garden City: Doubleday & Company, Inc., 1972.

Haney, William H. *The Mountain People of Kentucky.* Cincinnati: The Robert Clark Co., 1906.

Kellner, Esther. *Moonshine: Its History and Folklore.* Indianapolis: The Bobbs-Merrill Company, 1971.

Kephart, Horace. *Our Southern Highlanders.* New York: Outing Publishing Company, 1913.

Marshall, Humphrey. *The History of Kentucky.* 2 volumes. Frankfort: G. S. Robinson, 1824.

Montell, William Lynwood. *The Saga of Coe Ridge: A Study in Oral History.* Knoxville: The University of Tennessee Press, 1970.

A New English Dictionary on Historical Principles. Oxford: Clarendon, 1888.

Raine, James Watt. *The Land of Saddlebags: A Study of the Mountain People of Appalachia.* New York: Published jointly by Council of Women for Home Missions and Missionary Education Movement of the United States and Canada, 1924.

Smith, Z. F. *The History of Kentucky.* Louisville: Courier-Journal Job Printing Company, 1886.

Tapp, Hambleton. *A Sesqui-centennial History of Kentucky.* Edited by Frederick A. Wallis. 4 volumes. Louisville: The Historical Record Association, 1945.

United States Statutes at Large. Volumes 3 (1861) and 12 (1865). Boston: Little, Brown & Company.

Verhoeff, Mary. *The Kentucky Mountains: Transportation and Commerce 1750 to 1911.* Louisville: John P. Morton and Co., 1911.

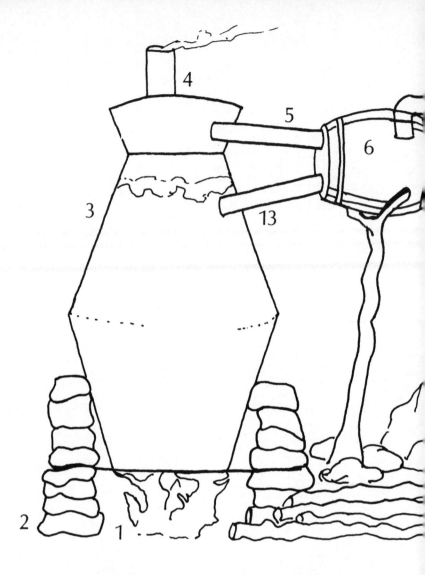

SCHEMATIC DESIGN FOR A POT STILL

1. Firebox for
   burning wood

2. Masonry furnace

3. Pot still

4. Smoke vent

5. Connection from
   still cap to puker

6. Puker

7. Connection from
   puker to thump-keg

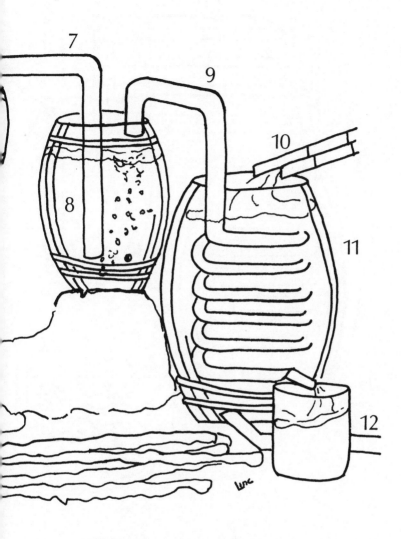

8. Thump-keg

9. Connection from
   thump-keg to
   flakestand

10. Cold water source
    for flakestand

11. Flakestand

12. Catch-can

13. Pipe to carry any
    mash that boils
    over back into the
    still

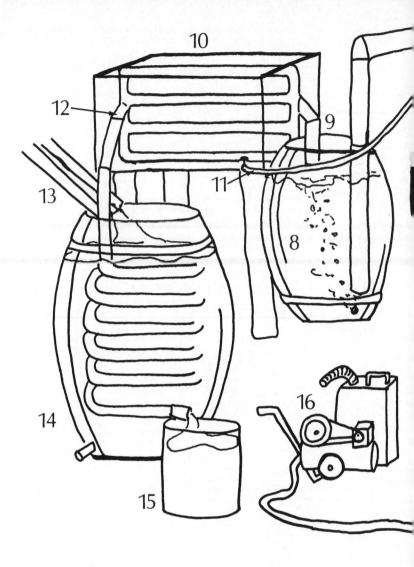

SCHEMATIC DESIGN FOR A STEAM STILL

1. Water source for boiler
2. Steam boiler
3. Firebox
4. Pressure burner
5. Steam still
6. Steam connection to still
7. Connection from still to thump-keg

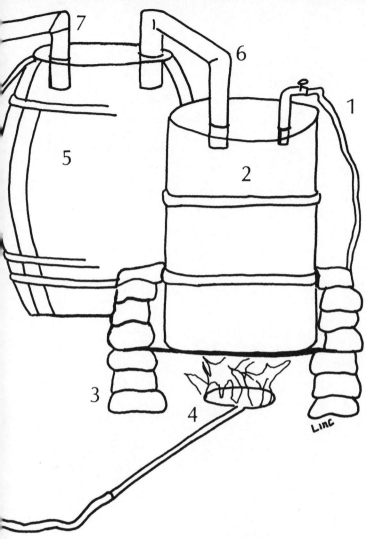

8. Thump-keg

9. Connection from thump-keg through heater-box

10. Heater-box

11. Hose to carry heated beer to still

12. Connection to flakestand

13. Cold water source for flakestand

14. Flakestand

15. Catch-can

16. Compressor for gasoline burner